John C. Thompson
Conway

June
, 1901.

Memories of
Davidson College

Air View of Davidson College Campus

Memories of
Davidson College

by

WALTER L. LINGLE

John Knox Press
RICHMOND · VIRGINIA

🦉 Foreword

In response to the gracious invitation of the Trustees and Administration of the college, I have written my memories of Davidson College, covering a period of more than fifty years, dating from my entrance into the college as a freshman in the fall of 1888. I have no idea whether I have come even within gunshot of what the Trustees and Administration had in mind. But when one goes to write his memories he can write only about things which he remembers.

Knowing the treachery of the human mind I have not been willing to trust my memory alone, but have carefully checked what I thought I remembered with the college records and publications. I have found it a pleasant employment even if it has involved considerable labor. It was pleasant to live over again the memories of these many years, and to be associated again in spirit with the students, members of the faculty, and trustees whom I have known and loved in years gone by, many of whom have gone on to their eternal reward. The words of Virgil come to mind: "Hæc olim meminisse juvabit."

If these memories should ever have any readers, I trust that they will find them neither uninteresting nor unprofitable. I also have a hope that they may be of service in helping to recall some of the history of the college in after years.

WALTER L. LINGLE

Davidson, North Carolina
January, 1947

🕭 Introduction

IT IS NO exaggeration to state that Dr. W. L. Lingle knows more about Davidson College than any living person. It is because of this fact, clearly recognized by the Davidson family, that we have asked him to set down for permanent record his memories of over a half-century of close personal association with the college. This association was, first, as a student, then as an alumnus, later as a trustee, then as President of the Trustees, as President of the college from 1929 to 1941, and now as President Emeritus, close neighbor, and always helpful friend.

Dr. Lingle possesses the all-too-rare quality of being interesting, whether it be in conversation, in teaching, in preaching, or in writing. It used to be noted in the years when he was Chairman of the Montreat Program that he could make routine announcements interesting. This quality is accompanied by a fine sense of humor. Both these qualities are manifest in this book, which is basically historical. The reader will not only know Davidson College better but will also find enrichment and stimulus in the process.

A significant phase of Dr. Lingle's equipment for the writing of this book is his broad and inspiring ministry in many places and areas. Born in Rowan County, not twenty-five miles from the site of Davidson College, he took both his A.B. and A.M. degrees from Davidson. He was graduated from Union Theological Seminary. He was married to Alice Merle Dupuy, a daughter of the Davidson College community, in 1900. After serving as pastor of the Rock Hill, South Carolina, Presbyterian Church, and the First Presbyterian Church of Atlanta, Georgia, he was called to the faculty of Union Theological Seminary in Richmond. He was thirteen years in that position. He then became President of the Assembly's Training School in Richmond, and gave five years of active leadership to that institution. He was Moderator of the General Assembly of the Presbyterian Church, U.S., in 1920. He was manager of the Southern Presbyterian Conference in Montreat from 1910 to 1924. He is a member of Phi Beta Kappa, and of Omicron Delta Kappa. He is the author of several books, and is a contributing editor for the

Christian Observer. He and Mrs. Lingle occupy their own home in Davidson and continue to be a delightful asset to the college and the community, and to the Church at large.

Generations to come will read *Memories of Davidson College* with interest and benefit. Here is a valuable contribution to an institution "where a good past predicts a better future."

J. R. Cunningham

❧ Contents

I 🎩 My First Commencement

My FIRST COMMENCEMENT at Davidson College changed the whole course of my life. It was the Davidson spirit that did it. That was in June, 1888, before I was a college student, and when I had given up all hope of ever getting a college education. The Davidson spirit has exercised a tremendous influence upon hundreds of boys in one way or another and changed their lives much as it did mine. That is why I am writing this chapter. It will require a bit of autobiography to explain what happened in my case.

I was brought up on a farm in the bounds of Thyatira Presbyterian Church in Rowan County, North Carolina, about nine miles west of Salisbury. Thayatira is especially noted for a Christian classical school which was founded there about the year 1785 by the pastor, Rev. Samuel E. McCorkle, D.D., and named Zion-Parnassus. That name was Dr. McCorkle's way of expressing his conviction that religion and learning should go hand in hand. The foundations of that noted school were still standing within half a mile of my home when I was a boy. Recently the Historical Society of North Carolina placed a marker just across the highway from my old home, pointing to the site of Zion-Parnassus.

This noted school was closed about 1807 because of the serious illness of Dr. McCorkle, but from time to time other schools were opened. The Scotch-Irish Presbyterians of that community believed in Christian education. In 1884 a new two-story school building was erected within fifty yards of Thyatira Church, and in September of that year a Christian classical school was opened, with Mr. John Newton Correll as principal. He was still a young man, a consecrated Christian and a good teacher. I entered that school on the first day, and began the study of Latin, Greek, and Algebra all at the same time. I was then fifteen. As I proceeded with these studies I hoped that I might get to college as soon as I was thoroughly prepared. But in a year and a half after the school opened my father died. He left us a two-hundred-acre farm, but very little money after expenses were paid. We had to get a living out of that farm for my mother, three unmarried sisters and a younger brother, and myself. As I was the oldest son at home, I had to take charge of the farm. All hope of ever getting to college vanished.

More than two years passed by and then one day in the midst of wheat harvest my former teacher, Mr. Correll, came to our home and invited me to go to the Davidson College commencement with him. I declined on the ground that I was needed in the harvest field, that I had no suitable clothes, and that I had no business at a Davidson College commencement anyway. But he evidently had designs on me, though I did not suspect it then, and as he insisted, I yielded.

I expected to feel like a fish out of water at a Davidson commencement. I was certain that the college students would snicker at a country bumpkin, but to my amazement they did not. On the contrary they were very friendly. Mr. Correll introduced me to quite a number of students. He even introduced me to seniors! I know now that an extraordinarily fine senior class graduated at the commencement of 1888. Some of those seniors actually talked with me and showed me around the college. I still remember some of the stories they told. Dugald N. McLauchlin, who afterwards became a distinguished minister in the Presbyterian Church, was a member of that class, and one of the best storytellers I ever heard. As one of the stories he told at that time is so true to life and apropos of many occasions it will bear repeating here.

Down in the Scottish section of North Carolina from which he came there was a Presbyterian church that had an extraordinarily conservative group of ruling elders. They did not want anything new. One elder especially seemed to have been born in the objective case, and when any change was suggested he always promptly said, "I object!" As the pastor had some new enterprises he wanted to propose at a meeting of the elders he prayed very earnestly about it in his opening prayer, and in his earnestness prayed that if there were any objectors a cohort of angels might come and bear them safely to the New Jerusalem. Whereupon, the old elder interposed: "I object!" A great many of us have met characters like that on church boards and even on college boards.

But let us get on with the commencement. In those days, Davidson College had a real commencement, beginning on Sunday and extending through the following Thursday. In these latter times when students no longer remain for a commencement which has been reduced to two days, but scatter to the four winds the moment their final examinations are over, it is interesting to note that in those days practically every student remained through the entire commencement period, and attended nearly all the exercises. The present-day student probably thinks that a statement like that should be referred to the Believe-It-Or-Not column. He would also probably want to know how the college could provide a program to cover five long days. Let me give you an outline of the program of the commencement that I attended in June, 1888.

On Sunday morning Dr. Walter W. Moore, the gifted preacher and professor in Union Theological Seminary in Virginia, preached the baccalaureate sermon. He was one of the most princely men and one of the most eloquent preachers that I ever knew. About six years later I studied Hebrew under him at the Seminary, and he meant more to me than anyone I have ever known outside of my own family. Dr. John L. Girardeau, Professor of Theology in Columbia Theological Seminary, preached the sermon before the Young Men's Christian Association on Sunday evening of commencement. He had made a great reputation as a preacher to Negroes in Charleston before he became a professor in Columbia Seminary. This fact gives some intimation of his popular gifts as a preacher. Both of these Sunday services were largely attended by students, townspeople, and visitors.

Monday was a day more or less free for social activities, of which I shall speak presently. On Monday night the seniors had their Class Day entertainment, a unique feature of which was music by the Jug Band, the like of which I had never seen before. The music was not as classical as that rendered by Davidson's Symphonic Band today, but it was lots of fun.

On Tuesday the Trustees held their annual meeting. Most of them were venerable-looking men with grey beards. They seemed to take themselves and their work very seriously. While they were meeting, the students and their invited guests were going ahead with their social activities. On Tuesday night the two literary societies had very interesting programs. Invited alumni made talks, and then the meeting was thrown open to visiting alumni who indulged in college reminiscences and told stories both new and old.

On Wednesday morning Dr. Kemp P. Battle, president of the University of North Carolina, delivered the Annual Oration in the Commencement Hall. On Wednesday night the Annual Junior Oratorical Contest was held. This was one of the high lights of commencement. Weeks before, each of the two literary societies had chosen three of its best speakers and groomed them for this contest, for it was a contest not only between the individual speakers, but between the societies. The six orators spoke for about fifteen minutes each, and each man did his best. It was a really exciting contest. Mr. Jasper K. Smith of the Eumanean Society won the prize, which was a handsome gold medal. In after years Mr. Smith became a distinguished minister in the Presbyterian Church.

The climax came on Thursday. It was graduation day. The Commencement Hall in Old Chambers Building, holding a thousand people, was filled. After the opening prayer, Mr. W. H. Baker of Jacksonville, Florida, who had the second highest grades in the class for the four years, delivered the salutatory oration. He afterward became a well-known lawyer and judge in Florida. Mr. S. R. McKee, who stood third in the class, delivered the philosophical oration. Mr. D. N. McLauchlin and Mr. Howard Banks, who were chosen for their speaking ability, delivered orations on subjects of their own choosing. Then came the awarding of diplomas, medals, and honors. Mr. Robert G. Sparrow, who was said to have made the highest grades ever made at Davidson up to that time, delivered the valedictory oration. That concluded the exercises proper. However, many students and their best girls remained over for social activities Thursday night.

Now let us look at what we have referred to as the social activities of commencement week. Many of the students invited their best girls to commencement. They usually came on Saturday and remained through the following Thursday. The boarding houses and many private homes were filled with visiting girls, many of whom were college students. Besides these were quite a number of attrac-

Campus Trees

tive girls of college age living in the town of Davidson. When a student invited his girl to commencement he immediately got busy making dates for her among his friends. So by the time she arrived she was all dated up. Most of these dates were what are called "blind dates" in these days.

The dates included attendance upon the various exercises noted above, breakfast parties, dinner parties at boarding houses, walks, and so forth. In those days students took girls to church, not only at commencement, but also during the session. They even took them to the Annual Oration, which was sometimes long and dry.

But the piece de resistance socially was a buggy ride. Students who could afford it hired horses and buggies from the local livery stable or from Charlotte for the commencement period. The buggies were of the H.M.T. (hold-me-tight) variety. Horses, buggies, and harness were groomed to the last inch. Ribbons representing the college colors, or fraternity colors, were tied around the buggy whips. A student would put his girl into one of these buggies and then dash off on a country road (the only kind we had in those days) at top speed. When they got out of sight they slowed down for conversation and small talk.

Those students who could not afford to hire horses and buggies took their girls for walks, or strolls. A favorite walk was along a little stream a quarter of a mile south of the college to a place known as "Lover's Leap." The place does not look so romantic now. The cemetery was a popular place for walks, especially by moonlight. In December, 1943, I met an elect lady in New Orleans who told me that she attended the commencement of 1892, the year my class graduated, and her most distinct recollection of the commencement was the fact that her date took her for a walk in the cemetery. She married a Southwestern University student.

The climax of the social life was reached on Thursday night of commencement. That was the night when each student took his best girl for a promenade on the campus and through the society and fraternity halls. There was always a breath of excitement centering around the student marshals and their best girls. Prior to commencement each of the two literary societies elected three marshals to serve throughout the commencement period. In addition to these marshals the societies alternated in electing a Chief Marshal. These places were much sought after. During the commencement these seven marshals in proper dress and gloves, with gold-headed canes, wore handsome silk or satin regalias. These regalias were circular in form and were worn around the shoulders. Thus draped they reached nearly to the marshals' knees. They were handsome affairs. Thus attired the marshals flitted to and fro during commencement week, seating the crowds and doing the honors. The Chief Marshal's regalia was especially handsome. It was the custom on that last Thursday night for the marshals to put their regalias over the shoulders of their best girls before starting out on the promenade. There was always a twitter of excitement as to who was going to get whose regalia. There was an unusual amount of curiosity as to who was going to get the Chief Marshal's regalia. One of the prized possessions of the Davidson library is the regalia which Dr. Walter W. Moore gave his best girl when he was a student marshal in 1877. So there was plenty of social life, plenty of excitement, and plenty of small talk in those olden days.

There was still another form of social life that has not been mentioned. Country people from miles around came to commencement. They came in two-horse wagons, buggies, and phaetons. The groves north of the president's house, south of the church, and back of Old Chambers Building were crowded with vehicles of all kinds. Men, women, and children came. They brought their lunches and spent the day. I have always wondered why they came. Perhaps it was the brass band. The Steele Creek brass band was usually secured to play on the campus for one or two days during commencement. A brass band generally drew a crowd in those days. Or it may be that most of those people came as to a sort of picnic. Crops were pretty well "laid by," and the people deserved a day or two off after months of strenuous work on the farm. I remember how they streamed through the Old Chambers Building and up to the cupola, where they could get the finest view in all this part of the country. At any rate they had just as good time as the students and their girls had with their dates, horses, buggies, and regalias.

Those are some of the things that I saw and heard at my first commencement. No wonder they made a deep and lasting impression upon a country youth. But of all the things that I saw, heard, and felt, the friendliness and cordiality of the students made the deepest impression on me. It never occurred to me that they would even speak to a green country boy. In fact, I thought that some of them might snicker. If they had or had been rude in any way, I would never have returned to Davidson College. I know now that friendliness has been a characteristic of Davidson students from the beginning to this good hour. It is a part of the Davidson spirit, and one of the finest assets of the college.

I had plenty to think about on my way home and after I got there. I had seen and caught something of the Davidson spirit as revealed in that commencement. Then came the resolve that the impossible would have to be done. Ways and means would have to be found by which I could go to Davidson College. But that is another story. Suffice it to say that I entered Davidson that fall, and that a year later my young brother, Thomas W. Lingle, joined me. That is what the spirit of Davidson as seen and felt in the commencement of 1888 did for me. The spirit of Davidson has left the same deep impression upon hundreds of other students and prospective students.

II 🎩 Davidson College in 1888

On SEPTEMBER 13, 1888, I entered Davidson College as a fresh-man. A description of the college as it was then will give us some idea of how far we have come during the intervening years. But before describing the college as it was in 1888 let me try to recon-struct it as it was in the beginning. After that, let us glance at a dream which our forefathers had. Then we can look at the college as I saw it in my student days.

The Original Quadrangle

In March, 1835, Concord Presbytery passed a resolution calling for the founding of a college. After that things happened rather rapidly. Proper committees were appointed. Within a very few months the present site was selected for the location of the college and 469 acres of land were purchased for $1,521.00, according to the minutes of Concord Presbytery. This large acreage was pur-chased because the Presbytery planned to establish a manual labor institution, in which students could earn part of their expenses and at the same time learn a useful occupation. The manual labor fea-ture was discontinued in a very few years as impracticable.

The site on this large farm which was actually chosen for the buildings was on the west side of the present campus, next to Main Street. Work on the buildings began in 1836, and the college opened on March 12, 1837. The original buildings formed a small quad-rangle, the lines of which can be traced by records and by buildings that are still standing.

The east side of the quadrangle consisted of four buildings in a row, running north and south. Starting where the Philanthropic Society Hall now stands and going north, the buildings on the east side were as follows: A two-story residence for a professor (later known as Tammany Hall), Elm Row, Steward's Hall, and the president's home. These were all built in a line and were of red brick. Steward's Hall was a two-story building and stood between Elm Row and the president's home, just west of the old Carnegie

Library which is now the Guest House. The first floor of Steward's Hall was used for a dining room. The second floor originally provided rooms for the steward and his family. The business of the steward was to look after the boarding department and to supervise the farm and the manual labor department.

The west side of the quadrangle consisted of Oak Row and three other quaint little dormitories like it, built in a line running north and south along what is now Main Street. These four dormitories with Elm Row made a total of five of these little dormitories in the original quadrangle.

The Old Chapel stood at the north end of the quadrangle. It was transformed into Shearer Hall in 1901. The Old Chapel faced south and had pillars in front very much like the Philanthropic and Eumanean Halls. The first floor was divided into classrooms. On the second floor there was a comfortable auditorium where morning chapel was held and where church services were conducted for nearly fifty years.

All the above buildings were erected during the years 1836-38. The Philanthropic and Eumanean Halls, at the south end of the quadrangle, were not erected until 1849. With their erection the original quadrangle was complete. There were also a few small outbuildings which were of no particular importance. That was Davidson College for the first twenty-two years. The founding fathers might have said of their college what Daniel Webster said of Dartmouth in his argument before the Supreme Court of the United States: "It is, sir, as I have said, a small college, and yet there are those who love it."

A Dream of Our Forefathers

On February 7, 1855, Mr. Maxwell Chambers, a wealthy merchant of Salisbury, North Carolina, died, and in his will left more than two hundred thousand dollars to Davidson College. He had been a friend of the college from the beginning. That was a very large sum of money in those days. It was too large for the little quadrangle. Our forefathers had a dream of a much greater college than was originally planned. A New York architect was employed and he drew plans for an entirely new set of buildings to be located around a quadrangle about a hundred and forty yards east of the original quadrangle. The new plans called for a college that would provide for the housing and teaching of a thousand students. The central building was to be named in honor of Maxwell Chambers. New life and enthusiasm came into the little college as it dreamed of greater things.

The central building of the new plan, known in after years as the Old Chambers Building, was completed in 1859, and the first recitations were held in it on January 6, 1860. It was a massive building of brick and stone, about two hundred and eighty feet long, with a cupola ninety feet high. There were imposing pillars in front. The building consisted of a central part, and a north wing and a south wing. The wings were three stories high. The first floor of the central part was used for classrooms and laboratories. On the second floor there was a large auditorium with a seating capacity of more than a thousand people. This auditorium was almost a perfect cube as to length, breadth, and height, and had the worst acoustics I have ever known in any building. There was no method of heating it in winter. The north and south wings contained dormitories for students and could comfortably house about one hundred and thirty students with two in a room.

The War Between the States put an end to the larger plans drawn by the New York architect and an end to the dreams of our forefathers. The Old Chambers was the only one of the buildings provided for in the larger plans that was ever erected. There it stood in its solitary grandeur for many years. It was completely destroyed by fire on November 28, 1921. Nor was any building of any kind erected on the campus between 1860 and 1890.

Before passing to another head let me cite some contemporary witnesses for some of the statements made above, especially statements about the original quadrangle. Dr. J. G. Ramsay of the class of 1841 made one of the addresses at the semi-centennial of the college in 1887. Dr. Ramsay was not only a beloved physician and an elder in the Third Creek Presbyterian Church in Rowan County, but was active in civic affairs. He represented his county in the

DR. JOHN R. CUNNINGHAM
PRESIDENT OF DAVIDSON COLLEGE

state senate and was a member of the Confederate Congress. In Dr. Ramsay's address we find this paragraph describing the college as it was when he was a student:

"Dr. Morrison [the first president] removed to the college and took possession of the brick building now occupied by Professor Martin at the north end of the row of buildings now nearest the old Chapel. Professor P. J. Sparrow occupied the house [Tammany] at the south end of the row, near the Philanthropic Hall. The Steward's Hall and a dormitory [Elm Row], both still standing, were the only intervening buildings. Two dormitories near the public road west of the old Chapel, and a storehouse beyond the road, constituted, with a few necessary outbuildings, the entire accommodations at that time [that is, when the first session began in March, 1837]. The foundations of the old Chapel had been laid, as we have seen, nearly a year before, but the superstructure was not finished until 1838 . . . The three dormitories containing four rooms each, and twelve in all, were furnished for four students to a room, thus forty-eight only of the sixty-odd students were properly domiciled . . . By the beginning of the fall session, however, two additional dormitories had been provided, thus furnishing rooms for about eighty students [four to a room]."

In 1845 Fayetteville Presbytery sent a committee to Davidson to study the new college in detail. The committee made a very full and interesting report. You will find it in the College Library. In the report this statement occurs: "The buildings of the institution are: three dwellings, one for the president and two for professors, five dormitories for students, each containing four rooms, a large building for a Steward's Hall, and the accommodation of his family; and another large building, which is used for a Chapel, and for recitation rooms, for holding meetings of the literary societies, and depositing their libraries . . . The estimated cost of all these buildings is twenty-five thousand dollars." We may add that many men gave their services and the services of their wagons and teams free of charge as they helped to erect these buildings, and thus kept the cost to a minimum.

Dr. Jethro Rumple, pastor of the First Presbyterian Church of Salisbury, North Carolina, of the class of 1850, also made a semi-centennial address. Dr. Rumple was a scholarly man and a writer of history. In his address we find this statement: "Under the direction of these gentlemen [the building committee], the Steward's Hall, the President's house—now constituting a portion of Professor Martin's residence—the language professor's house, now standing somewhat dilapidated near the Philanthropic Hall, and known by the sobriquet of Tammany, with four blocks of brick dormitories along the road on the West side of the campus, in a line with those still standing north of the Eumanean Hall, were erected. The Chapel, still standing in the campus, was not erected till later on, and religious services were conducted the first year in the dining room of the Steward's Hall."

One more quotation will give us information about the original buildings, and what became of some of them. Prof. J. R. Blake was connected with Davidson College from 1861 to 1885. From 1871 to 1877 he served as chairman of the faculty, or acting president. In his semi-centennial address he tells us something about the grounds and buildings as he knew them in 1861. After telling of the New York architect's plans for a greater Davidson, and of the erection of the Old Chambers Building at the approximate cost of $90,000 (the minutes of the Trustees say approximately $81,000), he continues: "Already the spirit of innovation which was to have swept away the old dormitories and other buildings, out of harmony with the new and splendid program devised for the future, had accomplished much of its work, removing many of the old land-marks along the street line of the campus, and in front of the Phi Hall and other parts of the grounds.

"The sweeping policy was to have carried away with it, also, all that still remains of the present 'Oak Row,' 'Elm Row,' and 'The Cedars,' till the Old Chapel would be left alone as a solitary monument of that quaint architecture which adorned these academic groves in earlier days. The Old Campus being thus obliterated and every obstruction removed, the eye of fancy was delighted with the vision of comfortable residences of the faculty and graceful halls for other purposes rising around the New Campus in tasteful proportions of the most modern architecture. Such is an outline of the picture which loomed up before the imagination of those hopeful, faithful old guardians of our College."

The College in 1888

When I entered college in 1888 all the buildings of the east side of the original quadrangle were still standing, namely, Tammany, Elm Row, Steward's Hall, and the president's home, which was then occupied by Col. W. J. Martin, professor of Chemistry. The only building remaining on the west side of the Quadrangle was Oak Row. The Old Chapel was still standing unchanged. The Philanthropic and Eumanean Society Halls still stood at the south end of the quadrangle as they do to this day. Old Chambers still stood there alone, apart from the other buildings. These buildings that I have mentioned were the only buildings on the campus in 1888. I may add here that Tammany was removed in 1901 and some of the material was used in the reconstruction of the Old Chapel into Shearer Hall that year. Steward's Hall was removed in 1909 and some of the material used in the construction of the Carnegie Library.

In 1888 the Campus was a meadow. In his report to the Trustees in 1889 the Bursar stated that he had received $135.17 for the hay mowed from the campus that year. In 1893 this resolution was adopted by the Trustees: "That we approve the proposed change of the campus from a meadow into a lawn and the purchase of a one-horse lawnmower." There were no hard-surfaced walks or drives on the campus. In fact, there were none in town. The main street was a country road that was thick with dust in summer and deep in mud in the winter. The town took a great step forward, in my student days, in making a sidewalk on the west side of Main Street, by laying two planks, about a foot wide, in parallel lines for several hundred yards. Thus two people could walk side by side, provided they could walk on planks only a foot wide.

Those were primitive days as we looked at the college and the town. They looked more primitive still when we went inside the college buildings. There was not a stick of furniture of any kind in the dormitory rooms. Students were warned in the catalogue to bring their bedding from home and were informed that they could buy furniture at reasonable prices from the local stores. Better still the student might be able to buy secondhand furniture left for sale by the class that had graduated the previous commencement. The secondhand furniture that I purchased was very primitive. I remember that the mattress which I purchased was much wider than the bed, and gave me no end of trouble.

There were no electric lights. We used kerosene lamps. In due time somebody invented a nickel-plated lamp, known as a student lamp, which was a considerable improvement over the glass lamps. Practically all rooms had fireplaces or grates. A few had stoves. But we had to buy our own wood, chop it into right lengths, and make our own fires. The catalogue advertised that you could buy wood for a dollar and a half a cord. The wood was usually in eight-foot lengths and had to be chopped to suit your particular fireplace. For the major part of the time I was in college I roomed in the south end of Oak Row, and my wood pile was between Oak Row and Main Street. In addition to all this we swept our own rooms and made our own beds, when they were made.

There were no water works, nor hot or cold showers, in those days. When a student wanted water for any purpose he had to go to the well and draw it. They had a pump for students in the Old Chambers Building, but sometimes it refused to work and sometimes it ran dry. If a student in Oak Row wanted a bath, he had to build a fire, go to the well and draw some water, pour it into a kettle, and put it on the fire. Then he had to get another bucket of water to cool the boiling water to the right temperature. There were no porcelain tubs in those days. We had portable tin tubs and they were none too large. Two buckets of water, one hot and one cold, generally constituted the bath. It is estimated that the college now uses about one hundred gallons of water per student each day. In my day that amount of water would have lasted the average student several weeks.

There were no laundries, in this community at least, in those days. Colored women did our laundry for about a dollar and a half a month. They came and got it and brought it back again. Sometimes they brought back things that we did not send out, and we had no insecticide.

There were no modern toilet facilities. Instead there was a row of wooden privies in the rear of the Old Chambers Building. One of the events of the year, when the students got the mob spirit, as they sometimes will, was burning "the bushes." Pine lumber made a great fire.

When I first entered college there was no infirmary, but a little later in that year two rooms in the north end of Elm Row were set apart and furnished as an infirmary. But those two rooms were not a drop in the bucket when measles struck the college in the late winter of my freshman year. So most of us just had measles in our own rooms. There were several cases of pneumonia and one death.

The college had no boarding department, but good board could be had in private boarding houses for nine dollars a month. Ten dollars was the top price. One or two clubs got the board down to as low as six dollars a month, but I am afraid that the meals were not well-balanced. However, we did not know anything about calories and vitamins in those days, and it did not make so much difference.

The classrooms were just as primitive as the dormitories. To begin with, they were dingy and not well lighted or ventilated. They were heated by stoves, sometimes underheated and at other times overheated. Nor can I recall a single classroom that had desks. I do recall that R. L. Wharton, who has since rendered such distinguished service in Cuba, and I sat on a long bench that was not fastened to the floor in the Greek room, and we sometimes worried Dr. Harding, in our forgetful moments, by rocking back and forth.

For fear that you will accuse me of exaggeration, let me quote a statement from the President's Report to the Trustees in June, 1892. It reads thus: "We need to have the recitation rooms refurnished throughout. Their present condition is a shame to any school that pretends to decency."

The current expenses of the college for the fiscal year 1888-1889, including the salaries of the president and professors, were $13,016.84. The income for current expenses from all sources was $12,487.95. The endowment was $108,047.10. No wonder that the dormitories and classrooms were no better furnished.

Yes, those were primitive days, but we loved them, and even after the lapse of more than half a century they still form one of the brightest spots in our memories. If you are inclined to find fault with those who are responsible for the well-being of the college, remember that we were not far removed from the War Between the States, which had impoverished the college and the whole South. Remember, too, that we had a great faculty, and nothing else mattered much.

III 🐾 The Faculty

DAVIDSON COLLEGE has always believed in having a strong faculty. The Trustees and Administration have evidently held to the conviction expressed by President Garfield in his famous saying about Mark Hopkins, namely, that the faculty is of more importance than buildings and equipment, as important as they may be. Perhaps it will be germane to our subject if we pause and look a little more closely at President Garfield's noted saying, of which there are several versions.

Mark Hopkins was the distinguished president of Williams College from 1836 to 1872. He was a great teacher and a great personality. It was said of him that he not only taught philosophy, but that he taught his students to philosophize. "What do *you* think?" was a question that he was forever putting to his students. Garfield graduated from Williams College in 1856. From that day until his death Mark Hopkins was his hero and intimate friend. In 1871 the Williams College alumni in New York had a banquet at Delmonico's. Garfield, who was then a leader in the United States Congress, was invited to be the principal speaker. Just before his address, another speaker gave a very gloomy picture of Williams College. He felt that they needed better buildings, new equipment, and a larger plant. Dr. Burke A. Hinsdale, president of Hiram College, in which Garfield had been a teacher and of which he was a trustee, tells us what followed in his book, *President Garfield and Education*, which was published in 1882, the year after Garfield was assassinated. Dr. Hinsdale was an intimate friend of Garfield from his youth up.

In his address, according to Dr. Hinsdale, Garfield said: "To all that has been said, I most heartily assent. No words of mine shall in any way detract from the importance of everything that has been urged; but I am not willing that this discussion should close without mention of the value of the true teacher. Give me a log hut, with only a simple bench, Mark Hopkins on one end and I on the other, and you may have all the buildings, apparatus, and libraries without him."

Garfield expressed the same idea the very next year in a letter to the Williams College Alumni Chapter in Boston, regretfully declining an invitation to speak at their meeting. He wrote: "So long as Williams College can offer salaries which will command and retain the best teaching talent of the country, she will offer a far greater attraction to thoughtful and ambitious students than any splendor of her architecture or richness of her cabinets and libraries. Such a college can bring the personal influence of its professors much more fully to bear on its students than can be done in a university. I believe, then, that the two great supports of the college are cheap bread and costly brains."

I have inserted these quotations because they express so clearly the convictions which our fathers and forefathers held with reference to Davidson College. They believed in good architecture, handsome buildings, and up-to-date equipment, as shown by the fact that when they came into possession of the Maxwell Chambers legacy they employed a New York architect and instructed him to draw plans for larger and more beautiful buildings. The Old Chambers, which was a noble building, was a proof of their belief in good architecture. But when the War Between the States swept away most of the assets of the college and impoverished its supporters, and there was no money for both buildings and faculty, our fathers and forefathers never hesitated. They let buildings go and put all they had into the faculty. That is why they had dingy buildings and poor equipment, but a good faculty, in my student days.

Davidson still holds to that ideal. There are several handsome buildings now, but Davidson continues to put the ability, character, and personality of her faculty before buildings and equipment. While I was president of Davidson one of the well-known Educational Foundations sent a committee to study a number of southern institutions. The members of the committee had been on the Davidson campus a day or two before I was aware of their presence. They had purposely refrained from coming to the president's office until they had learned something of the college in a firsthand way from other sources. Then they came to my office. The thing that had impressed them most about Davidson was the faculty. The main

Philanthropic Society Hall

President's Home

Eumanean Society Hall

question they wanted to ask me was how we proceeded to secure such a splendid faculty from the point of view of ability, personality, and character. I replied that we sought for them until we found them. Then I added that there are three questions that we ask as a minimum about every prospective professor: Does he know his subject? Can he teach it? Are his character and personality such as will enable him to have a positive Christian influence in the classroom and on the campus?

But as I am writing memories it is high time for me to come to the faculty that was here in 1888, and that remained without a change for the next five years. There were only seven members of the faculty, and one student instructor who taught preparatory mathematics. Only one of the seven had been connected with the Davidson faculty for more than five years. Two of them came as new members of the faculty in the fall of 1888. The youngest member of the faculty was twenty-seven years of age, the next youngest was twenty-eight, and the third was thirty. All these young men were full professors. They did not know anything about associate or assistant professors at Davidson in those days. The oldest member of the faculty was fifty-eight. The president was fifty-six. Fully aware of the fact that one's own personal equation makes it impossible for him to make a perfect appraisal of another, I shall now undertake to tell something of each member of the faculty as I knew them in my student days and afterwards. I shall name them in order of their respective ages.

Colonel W. J. Martin, professor of Chemistry, was the Nestor of the faculty. He came to Davidson in 1870, and notwithstanding numerous flattering offers to go elsewhere, remained at Davidson until his death in 1896. He was one of the most forceful personalities and one of the best teachers I have ever known.

Colonel Martin was born in Richmond in 1830, graduated from the University of Virginia, taught three years in Washington College, Pennsylvania, and then came to the University of North Carolina, as professor of Chemistry, in 1857. He entered the Confederate army in 1861 and went through the entire war until the surrender at Appomattox. He was in many battles, including Gettysburg, was wounded four times, was made a colonel, and finally was made a general just prior to the surrender. At the close of the war he returned to the University of North Carolina and remained there several years until the University was closed by Reconstruction agencies. After that he came to Davidson.

As was perfectly natural, Colonel Martin always retained something of the military air about him in his bearing and in his teaching. When he made announcements in chapel or in class they sounded very much like military orders. At times he seemed almost curt. This might have been objectionable except for the fact that there was always a twinkle in his left eye as he gave orders. An incident will illustrate this.

In connection with my graduation in 1892 I had to make a speech in that big auditorium in Old Chambers. There were hundreds of people present and I was so frightened that my knees trembled. As there was no stand to hold to, I walked back and forth to keep the audience from observing my trembling knees. When commencement was over I went by Colonel Martin's home to say good-bye. I had no intention of sitting down or staying for more than a moment. His greeting ran about this way: "Sit down, sir. Did you ever go to a circus?" When I answered in the affirmative he inquired: "At the circus did you ever see a bear tethered to a stake and watch him go back and forth all day long?" When I replied that I had, he said: "That's you, sir. That's exactly the way you did in making your graduation speech. If you can't stand still perhaps you had better go home to your mother and stay there." All the while his left eye was twinkling. Then he told me good-bye with a warm handclasp that told me something of the warmth of his heart and his deep interest in my well-being. That was the best lesson in public speaking I ever had. Even to this day when I begin to walk around in the pulpit I think of Colonel Martin and the tethered bear.

I am going to let another tell you about Colonel Martin as a teacher. In October, 1913, the Presbyterian Synod of North Carolina celebrated the centennial of its organization with quite a number of addresses. Dr. C. Alphonso Smith, who was then professor of English at the University of Virginia, but had graduated at Davidson in 1884, made an address on Presbyterians in Educational Work in North Carolina from 1813 to 1913. In the address he spoke of several great Presbyterian teachers who lived during that period. Colonel Martin was one of them.

Of Colonel Martin he said: "Of all the college professors under whom it has been my lot to sit, my heart and head yield first place to William J. Martin. As a teacher it was not his scholarship that made the deepest impression, though his scholarship was ample and constantly renewed. It was first of all his ability to distinguish with lightning rapidity between the essential and the non-essential. He pierced instantly to the center of a subject, and expounded it from the center outward, and not from the circumference inward . . . But I am sure that I speak for all those who knew Colonel Martin when I say that the man was greater than the professor. He taught Chemistry professionally. He impressed manhood unconsciously."

Dr. J. B. Shearer, who was president of Davidson College from 1888 to 1901, was the next oldest member of the faculty. He was a large man with a noble head, a clean-shaven upper lip, and a chin beard. As he walked down the street with dignity, dressed in a Prince Albert coat, and with a cane, he made a very impressive figure. If he had walked along Fifth Avenue, New York, strangers would have taken notice of him and known that he was a man of importance.

Dr. Shearer was born in Appomattox County, Virginia, in 1832, graduated from Hampden-Sydney College, the University of Virginia, and Union Theological Seminary. He was the pastor of the Presbyterian Church at Chapel Hill, North Carolina, from 1858 to 1862; and of the church at Halifax, Virginia, from 1862 to 1870. From 1870 to the end of his life he gave himself with devotion to Christian education. From 1870 to 1879 he was president of Stewart College at Clarksville, Tennessee. Stewart College later became Southwestern Presbyterian University. Later still it was moved to Memphis and is now the Southwestern College. From 1879 to 1888 he was a professor in the Southwestern Presbyterian University. From there he came to Davidson.

The most distinctive thing that Dr. Shearer did for Davidson College was to introduce thorough courses in the English Bible covering three whole years, and to raise those courses to a college level. The Bible had been taught at Davidson College from the beginning, but the courses were very much of the nature of Sunday school lessons. Very few if any of these courses were required. From Dr. Shearer's day to this, two years of English Bible have been required for graduation. His influence resulted in the placing of courses in the English Bible in a number of church-related colleges.

Dr. Shearer also rendered a fine service for the college by visiting churches, presbyteries, and synods and stirring up renewed interest in Christian education in general and in Davidson College in particular. No man in our Church has ever done more than he in promoting interest in Christian education throughout the Church.

It is interesting to learn from the records how hard Dr. Shearer labored to establish a great South-Atlantic Presbyterian university. His ideal was that every local church of sufficient size should have a parochial school, every presbytery should have a high school, every synod should have a college, and the whole system should be crowned by a great university. His dreams were never realized. Public schools of all grades and state-supported colleges and universities made it impossible. Perhaps it is just as well. Our Church has more colleges today than it can support. It would be little short of tragedy if in addition we had a university to support.

In addition to being president, Dr. Shearer taught the courses in English Bible. He knew the Bible in detail, and his courses were comprehensive and thoroughgoing. Articles in the *Davidson Monthly,* a student publication of that era, praised the courses very highly. Dr. Shearer's method of teaching was dogmatic. Sometimes he substituted ridicule and sarcasm for argument. This was especially true when he came to the subject of Higher Criticism. With all of his ability, I am not sure that he knew that Higher Criticism is a method and not a result. He did not follow the method of Mark Hopkins in asking the student: "What do *you* think?" At any rate, I cannot remember having done much thinking.

DR. WALTER LEE LINGLE

PRESIDENT EMERITUS OF DAVIDSON COLLEGE

Dr. and Mrs. Shearer had warm hearts and a deep interest in the students. They were always holding out both hands in helpfulness to students who were in need or in distress of any kind. He was not an enthusiastic believer in orphanages. Instead he believed that Christians should take the orphans of other Christians into their homes and give them a Christian home life, and that the state should provide for the orphans of non-Christians. He showed his faith by his works in always having one or two orphans in his home. He had no children of his own. When the Presbyterian Synod of North Carolina met at the Barium Springs Orphanage to dedicate a new building, Dr. Shearer was asked to make the dedicatory prayer. To the amazement of everybody he prayed for twenty-seven minutes. In those days the brethren stood for prayer, but that day they sat down, one after another, until the last one, Dr. Peyton H. Hoge, went down. As Dr. Shearer always prayed with his eyes open he must have seen what was happening, but it did not shorten the prayer. I could not understand this until several years afterward, when he explained to me that Dr. W. P. Jacobs, of the Thornwell Orphanage, who made the address on that occasion, had promulgated some heresies about orphanages that needed to be corrected.

It was said that Dr. Shearer was close in a trade, and that he accumulated a considerable estate. If so, he was always generous with his money to those in need and to the institutions and agencies of the Church, and when he died he had very little left. Upon his death there were many to rise up and call his name blessed.

Professor W. S. Graves occupied the chair of Latin and French during my student days. He was a Virginia gentleman of the old school. Better still, he was a cultured, Christian gentleman. Shortly after I entered college there came an invitation to me and several other freshmen to take supper in his home. I remember that I went with a good deal of trepidation for I was not sure that I would know how to act. It was the first time I was ever in a professor's home. But the professor and his charming wife soon put us at ease. Thereafter I always had a warm spot in my heart for them.

Professor Graves was born near Charlottesville, Virginia, in 1848. He graduated from Washington College while General Lee was president. After that, he taught for several years and then studied law. He practiced law in Richmond and Bedford from 1872 to 1883, and then decided that he wanted to be a teacher of languages. He studied at Johns Hopkins under the distinguished Dr. Gildersleeve. In 1885 he was elected professor of Greek and German at Davidson College. After teaching for a year at Davidson he returned to Johns Hopkins for a year on leave of absence in order to complete the work for his doctor's degree. He failed to receive the coveted degree, whereupon the Davidson Trustees expressed deep concern. Upon his return to Davidson in the fall of 1887 he was transferred to the chair of Latin and French. As might be guessed from the above sketch, although he was a fine Christian gentleman, he was not a very successful teacher. He began to specialize on Greek, Latin, French, and German too late in life.

I recall that he had a quiet sense of humor and sometimes got off a Latin joke or pun in class. One day our class conspired together and decided that we would not laugh at his next Latin joke. The next joke centered about the Latin phrase "ne quid nimis." When he had finished we sat as solemn as if we had been at a prayer meeting. He paused for a moment and then intimated that it was rather hard on a professor to tell a joke and then have to furnish the brains to see the point. He resigned and left Davidson in 1893 with the high esteem of all who knew him.

Dr. W. D. Vinson was professor of Mathematics at Davidson from 1880 until his death in 1897. He had as much of what Scotsmen call primordial brain power as any man I ever knew. He had a remarkable mind both as to memory and reasoning powers. His method of teaching was akin to the method followed by Mark Hopkins. In quizzing his students he was not satisfied with an answer from the textbook. "What do *you* say?" was his standing question. He taught his students to think.

Dr. Vinson was born in 1849 in the Richland District of South Carolina. At the tender age of five he was left an orphan by the death of his mother and father. The story of his struggles for an education in his boyhood days would make a thrilling chapter in biography. He graduated from Washington and Lee University in 1871, taking all the honors and medals that were offered. Among other honors he won the Robinson prize medal in Latin, Greek, and Mathematics. That shows something of his versatility. He was also at home in French and German.

After graduation he taught for a number of years in Texas, notably in Austin College, Sherman, where he made quite a reputation as a teacher. From there he came to Davidson. When I entered Davidson in 1888 he was regarded as one of the most popular and one of the ablest teachers here. In those days we were required to take two years of Mathematics. In the two years I was so deeply impressed by the man and the teacher, that, although I was a candidate for the ministry, I continued in Mathematics until I had taken all the courses he offered. They said that it would be good for the mind. Be that as it may, he left an indelible impression upon me not only by his teaching but by his whole personality.

Dr. Vinson was deeply religious, but as free from cant as any man I have ever known. He taught a class of students every Sunday morning. I still remember a class he taught using as his textbook *The Early Days of Christianity* by Dean F. W. Farrar. It was a very illuminating course.

In connection with Dr. Vinson I like to think of an incident a fellow student who roomed near me told me. One winter night while Dr. Vinson was at home alone, this student, not best known for his piety, was invited to spend the night with him. They slept in the same room. The student, getting ready first, hopped into bed without saying the prayers his mother had taught him. When Dr. Vinson was ready for bed he knelt down devoutly, as was his custom, and said his prayers. The student's conscience smote him. He got out of bed, knelt down by his teacher, and remained there until the prayer was ended. That incident gives some intimation of the kind of religion Dr. Vinson had, and the kind of influence he had upon his students.

Dr. William Spenser Currell was professor of English during my student days. In fact, he was the first whole-time professor of English in the history of the college. Prior to his coming, there were brief courses in English taught by professors in other departments.

He and Dr. Walter W. Moore of Union Theological Seminary were the two most inspiring teachers I ever had.

Dr. Currell was born in Charleston, South Carolina, in 1858, graduated from Washington College, and took his doctor's degree from that institution in 1882, after it had become Washington and Lee University. From 1882 to 1886 he was professor of English, Logic, and Political Economy in Hampden-Sydney College. In 1886 he came to Davidson as professor of English, Psychology, and Political Economy and remained at Davidson until 1895, when he went to Washington and Lee as professor of English. Later still he became president of the University of South Carolina.

In 1887 Psychology and Political Economy were dropped from his title and he was listed thereafter in the catalogue as professor of English. However, I remember mighty well that I took a course in Logic under him, and a course in Green's Short History of the English People, which was called short just for fun. But he gave most of his time and energy to courses in English, of which there were quite a number.

Dr. Currell was an animated, vivacious sort of man and teacher, and threw the whole of his energies into his teaching. Some professors sat down while teaching, but not Dr. Currell. He was up and on the move. He was a very friendly man, and took a deep interest in the individual student. Sometimes you would see him walking down the street arm in arm with a freshman, chatting away on even terms with him. Yet there was a dignity about him which intimated to the student that he could go so far and no farther. He never courted popularity, and yet he became one of the most popular, if not the most popular, members of the faculty. Sometimes he seemed to court unpopularity, especially in reporting students for breach of college regulations.

Take this instance, for example. He lived in the brick house just across Main Street from the President's home. As it was a large house for a small family, he rented a front room on the first floor to Hay Watson Smith, who was then a student. On one occasion when Dr. and Mrs. Currell had a number of young ladies visiting them, the student string quartet slipped into Mr. Smith's room one night to give the young ladies a serenade. In those days it was against the rules for a student to leave the campus after seven o'clock in the evening without permission. Dr. Currell knew that the members of the quartet were violating the rule, so he knocked on Mr. Smith's door with a view to getting their names. Mr. Smith refused him entrance. Dr. Currell insisted that it was his house. Mr. Smith insisted just as strenuously that it was his room, and the door was never opened. The members of the quartet later sent Dr. Currell their names and took their demerits. It always struck me that the professor let his conscience carry him to an extreme on that occasion. At times even a professor should, like the proverbial Japanese monkey, see nothing, hear nothing, and say nothing.

Dr. Currell took a great interest in the young people of the town and conducted a regular Chautauqua course for them. He also had a Poetry League for those young people who wanted to study and memorize some of the choicest poetry. Even to this day I hear some of that poetry quoted by an elect lady in our home, who was a young lady in the town of Davidson in those days.

Dr. Henry Louis Smith was listed in the catalogue as professor of Natural Philosophy in my student days. He taught Physics, Geology, Mineralogy, Astronomy, and Meteorology. He was also an inspiring teacher. His vocabulary was so vivid that he could make a student almost see an atom or molecule with the naked eye. The course in Physics under him was one of the most illuminating courses I ever took.

Dr. Smith was born in Greensboro, North Carolina, in 1859. He was a member of one of the most distinguished families the state has ever produced. Graduating from Davidson in 1881 he taught in a classical school at Selma, North Carolina, for five years. After that he did graduate work at the University of Virginia and later received his doctor's degree. He came to Davidson in 1887 and served as professor of Physics and other subjects until 1901. In that year he was elected president of Davidson and held that office until 1912, when he became president of Washington and Lee University.

An item in the *Davidson Monthly* in October, 1887, gives the key to Dr. Smith's work at Davidson. It reads thus: "Our only objection to Professor Smith is that since he is such a hard worker himself and has always been accustomed to doing his duty, he expects us to do the same." That was written when he had been connected with the college less than two months. The students had gotten his number. He was always a hard worker, always doing his duty and more, and always expecting his students to do the same.

The nickname which the students gave him was significant. They called him "Project." He was always full of new ideas for his own department and for the college as a whole. As far as money would allow he kept his own department up to date.

There is space to tell only of some of the things he did during my student days. As Superintendent of Grounds and Buildings he changed the campus from a meadow into a lawn, and did much to improve the upkeep of the buildings. He took the lead in raising the money for Morrison Hall, which was said to be the first college Y.M.C.A. building in the South. It was the only building of any kind erected on the Davidson campus between 1860 and 1900. He also conceived the idea of having a lake where students could boat and swim and skate, and took the lead in raising the money and in the building of Lake Wiley, which was located northeast of the college on the area that is now partly covered by the golf course. Unfortunately the dam was washed away, but we had lots of fun while it lasted. These are just a few illustrations of the directions the energies of this young professor took. No wonder that in due time he became president of Davidson and afterwards of Washington and Lee.

Dr. C. R. Harding came to Davidson as professor of Greek and German in 1888, the year that my class entered as freshmen, and he still abides to this good day (1947). Although he was made professor emeritus in 1934, he continued to teach certain elective courses until 1944. Thus he served the college for fifty-six years, a longer time by far than anyone else ever connected with it.

Dr. Harding was born in Charlotte, North Carolina, in 1861, graduated from Davidson in 1880, took graduate work at Johns

Hopkins, was professor of Greek in Hampden-Sydney College 1883-85, and took his doctor's degree at Johns Hopkins in 1887, under Dr. Gildersleeve, the great teacher of Latin and Greek. In September, 1888, he came to Davidson College with his bride.

I took four years of Greek under Dr. Harding, beginning with Lysias and ending with Euripides, Sophocles, and the clouds of Aristophanes. It seems to me that we must have read all the Greek extant. In those days we were expected to have had about two years of Greek before entering college. Dr. Harding never claimed to be a great teacher, but he was a good teacher for those who really wanted to learn Greek. In the meantime he has been a cultured Christian gentleman, and has influenced one generation of students after another for good.

In his earlier years students were inclined to tease Dr. Harding. For instance, on the first of one April they put a number of alarm clocks in the empty stove in his classroom, set to go off one after another. You can imagine the pandemonium that ensued. That and many other things of a similar nature they did, and he did not know exactly how to cope with them. He took their pranks good-naturedly and remonstrated with them in a Christian spirit. That only gave the students a zest for more pranks. His predecessor, Dr. Gonzales Lodge, who was a temporary supply in the Greek chair, took a more excellent way. He was a young man and was trying to sprout a mustache. One morning as he entered the Greek room he observed a number of verses of doggerel on the board, making sport of his mustache. He said nothing until class was over and he was making assignments for the next recitation. He concluded the assignment thus: "You will find on the board the English for the next Greek composition." And that class had to put the whole of the doggerel into Greek. A professor like that can always outsmart students who are inclined to play pranks. But the students ceased to play pranks on Dr. Harding long ago. They have a great respect for him. In fact, he is no longer a mere individual, but an institution.

There formerly stood, immediately in front of the residence now occupied by Dr. Harding, a dilapidated residence known as Old Danville. In June, 1889, the Trustees gave instructions to tear down

Old Danville and erect a residence for Dr. Harding, using as much of the old material as possible. In 1890 the Executive Committee reported to the Trustees that Old Danville had been torn down and a residence for Dr. Harding had been erected at a cost of $825. Dr. and Mrs. Harding had already moved into the residence, which is located just across Main Street from the president's home. That was in 1890, mind you, and they have lived there ever since. As other residences became vacant they could have moved into a much more comfortable home, but they have preferred to remain right there. When I see them there I think of the poem by Sam Walter Foss, "The House by the Side of the Road," based on lines from Dr. Harding's own beloved Homer:

> "He was a friend to man, and he lived
> In a house by the side of the road."

* * * * *

Those were the members of the faculty as I knew them from 1888 to 1892. I have seen a good many faculties since, but none that ranks higher in my thinking than that one.

IV ❦ Students and Student Life

REMEMBERING THAT a college exists for its students and the influence which they may have upon the world, let us now look at the student life and the students as I knew them in my college days and afterwards.

My class, consisting of twenty-nine members, entered Davidson as freshmen in September, 1888. To be specific, it was September 13, but it was not Friday. As I look back over the years and as I look at the old photographs, I am sure that it must have been a very verdant class. Not only so, but my own verdancy must have been outstanding. At any rate, Dr. Harding remembered nearly forty years later how green I was. It was on this wise:

In 1927 the faculty presented the Trustees with a rather lengthy paper recommending that the qualifications for the A.B. degree be changed so that a student might win it by taking a certain number of hours in Ancient *or* Modern Languages along with his other studies. That meant that a student could get the A.B. degree without taking Greek or Latin.

Dr. Harding, professor of Greek, became alarmed. He felt that the faculty recommendations sounded the death knell of Greek and Latin. He asked for the privilege of addressing the Trustees. In his opening remark he expressed the hope that none of the trustees would take that paper from the faculty seriously. I was presiding, and replied that I did, meaning that the trustees should take any communication from the faculty seriously. He lit on his feet, as quick as a cat. Looking at me, he said, "I am amazed that of all people you should say that." Then he pictured me as he remembered me as a green freshman in the fall of 1888. It was some picture. After that he told how I took four years of Greek, and ever so many years of Latin. Having done that, he pictured me as I was in 1927, and told of the various positions that I had held. Greek and Latin had wrought the transformation. His two pictures were before and after taking . The Trustees declined to approve the faculty recommendation.

· 39 ·

I saw Dr. Henry Louis Smith, while he was president of the college, do something like that at the commencement in 1905. He was introducing Mr. S. Clay Williams, who has since attained national distinction in the business and political world. Mr. Williams was graduating at the head of his class, and had won every medal in sight, and Dr. Smith was introducing him as Valedictorian. He told of all the honors he had won and what a wonderful fellow he was. Having done that, he told the audience that they should have seen how green he was when he entered college as a freshman. The college had made all the difference!

It is just here that the college professor has his greatest reward. After a professor has taken his doctor's degree and explored worlds that the average student has never dreamed of, it is a terrible letdown to have to teach freshmen the very rudimentary principles of the subject. Instead of being an intellectual stimulus, it is an intellectual letdown. There is a lot of drudgery in the average college professor's life. But when he sees the transformation that takes place in the lives of crude freshmen in the space of four years, and feels that maybe he had a little part in it, he has his reward.

The total number of students in 1888 was ninety-six, which was smaller than average. Between 1868 and 1888 the average attendance was one hundred and eight. In 1887 there were only eighty-nine students. The slump was due mainly to the fact that Dr. Luther McKinnon, who was elected president in 1885, was stricken with an illness that put him out of commission a very few months after his election, and there was no one to keep up the public contacts. He resigned, but the Trustees did not accept his resignation until 1888 when it was clear that he was permanently incapacitated. Even prior to Dr. McKinnon's illness there had been some friction between the faculty and the Trustees, and some of the members of the faculty, including President Hepburn, resigned. However, with the coming of Dr. Shearer as president in 1888, student attendance began gradually to increase.

If you want to know what manner of students we were in those days, turn to the January-February *Davidson Monthly* for 1892. In November, 1891, Dr. Henry Louis Smith, always overflowing with new ideas, sent to every student an elaborate questionnaire, containing twenty-nine questions. Two-thirds of the students filled out and returned the questionnaire, which was about themselves. Dr. Smith compiled the information thus gathered, and prepared the article for the *Davidson Monthly*. Here are a few of the facts.

The average student in November, 1891, was approximately twenty-two years of age. The youngest was fifteen and the oldest twenty-eight. Forty-eight per cent of them were qualified to vote. The tallest student was six feet three and three-quarters inches. The shortest was five feet three inches. The average weight was 148 pounds. The heaviest was 296 and the lightest 110.

The most popular forms of exercise were football, tennis, base-ball, and skating. At that time roller-skating was very popular with the students and the young ladies of the town. Three per cent of the students liked dancing best. The studies liked best were Physics, Bible, English, and Math. The study liked least was Metaphysics.

Fifty-two per cent visited the young ladies of the town. Forty-two per cent belonged to fraternities and ninety-five and one-half per cent belonged to the Literary Societies. Eighty per cent had decided upon their lifework or had a preference. The largest number were planning to be ministers, physicians, and lawyers. Sixty-two per cent were teetotallers, twenty-seven per cent smoked, twenty-three per cent chewed, and some of these did both. Fifty-eight per cent thought that profanity was the most prevalent sin on the campus. Other sins were idleness and neglect of duty. One per cent thought that self-conceit was the most prevalent sin. According to the student vote, the strongest moral character on the campus was C. M. Richards, which is another proof that the boy is father to the man.

In response to the question concerning the greatest need of the college, there were thirty-six different needs mentioned, going to show that the needs of the college in those days were *many*. Among those mentioned most frequently were: water works, electric lights, a new chapel, modern improvements in general, a chair of elocution and music, more athletics, and of course a few suggested a new faculty, forgetting that the one we had was almost brand-new.

If you want to know how we behaved in those days, I refer you to the reports made by President Shearer to the Trustees at the close of each academic year. In 1889 he reported: "The faculty is hopeful and harmonious, and the students orderly, diligent and enthusiastic." In 1890 he reported: "The session in the main has been a quiet and orderly one, and much good work has been done." In 1891 he reported: "The session has been in the main an orderly one, though not entirely free from disagreeable incidents. There have been two cases of serious discipline during the year, and there no doubt would have been more if certain disorders could have been located." That does not sound quite so good. I cannot recall just what the disorders were.

As I read his next report my heart swells with pride, for it is concerning the year in which we—I mean my class—were seniors. In that year he reported: "The session has been characterized by extraordinarily good order and devotion to duty. There has been nothing like it in the history of the college, so far as the experience of the present faculty goes. The entente cordiale between students and faculty, and the general tone of the student body, has made the year's work a pleasure to all parties."

Dr. Shearer must have been a golden-hearted man, or else he had a good forgettery. When he made that glowing report in 1889 he seems to have forgotten that the students had burned him in effigy in the spring of that year. Two popular students were suspended from the college for two weeks by the faculty for going to Charlotte without permission. The students blamed it on Dr. Shearer. They should have heard a wise remark that Dean Sentelle made a few years ago. When Dr. Richards and I voted for leniency in a case of discipline, Dean Sentelle remarked: "When a man has once been a pastor he has developed a pastor's heart, and is no longer qualified to administer discipline." Well, Dr. Shearer had a pastor's heart. If the students had known that they would not have held him responsible for the suspension of those two students.

At any rate, certain students made a man of straw, saturated it with kerosene, and hung it in front of Dr. Shearer's house, and just as prayer meeting adjourned at the church, they set fire to it. And then over on the campus they sang: "Hang John Bunyan [that was his name] on a sour apple tree," to the tune of "John Brown's Body." It was a disgraceful affair. Although I was a freshman and was not eligible to have a part in it even if I had wanted to, I have always been ashamed of it.

When you read his rosy reports remember that the president of a college does not always know all that is going on. The superintendent of grounds and buildings is usually better informed. In 1891 he made his report: "The entire damage account has reached the sum of $230.00 as will be seen from the accompanying statement." A better view of the total amount expended can be gotten from the bursar's account, about $525. Thus you see that there was quite a good deal of wanton destruction of property going on. The most of it was done by a few students of the baser sort, but I do not remember that the better element did anything to stop it.

I used to think that the destruction of college property was a tradition that belonged to Davidson exclusively, but it has been of more or less comfort to learn that it is a tradition in many colleges. In reading that charming book by Bliss Perry, *And Gladly Teach,* I ran across a passage in which he tells of the destruction at Williams College when he was a student there. We think of Williams as the last word in New England gentility and culture. He tells how students kicked ash cans and water pails down the stairways, and how they smashed window panes. He also tells how the old college carpenter, named Clark, defined a college student as "a window-breaking animal." To get comfort out of that is like a story in the *Reader's Digest.* When it was reported to a farmer that a cloud-burst had swept over his bottom land and drowned all his hogs he inquired: "Did it drown Tom Jones' hogs too?" "Yes." "Did it drown John Brown's hogs too?" "Yes." "Well, it's not as bad as I first thought."

Nor did the president, while saying those handsome things about us in his reports, know of an incident on the campus that came near being high tragedy. One spring a Negro baseball team in Concord challenged the Negro team in the town of Davidson for a game. They asked permission to play on the college diamond, and got it.

The diamond was located south of the Chambers Building where the Library and Science buildings now stand. I had a grandstand seat at a window on the second floor of Old Chambers where I could see everything that was going on. The game went beautifully for a while, but unfortunately a Negro spectator from Concord got in front of a hot-tempered student from the town of Davidson. The student ordered him to get out of his line of vision. As he didn't move promptly the student cut him with a riding whip. He got out of the way and said nothing, but another Negro took it up and used some abusive language to the student, and made as if he was ready to fight. The student drew his pistol. The Negro ducked into the crowd with the student right after him with drawn pistol. He did have sense enough not to shoot into the crowd. As the Negro emerged from the crowd he was right under the window where I sat, with the student a few paces behind. When the student was immediately under my window he fired at the Negro, who was running in the direction of the Richardson athletic field. Fortunately he missed him, but that Negro must have heard that bullet twice, when it passed him and when he passed it. In the meantime pandemonium reigned supreme. Some students got hold of the baseball bats and were swinging them right and left. The field was soon cleared and nobody was really hurt. Later the Concord team sent a friendly Davidson Negro to the students asking if they might have their bats and sweaters. The request was speedily granted and the incident was closed. But it might have been terrible, and all on account of a hot temper. The relationship between the students and the Negroes of the town of Davidson has always been friendly so far as my memory and observation go.

One more incident concerning this phase of student life will suffice. It is known as the "Trunk Tragedy." Examinations were held twice a year, just prior to the Christmas holidays and at the end of the session. When the schedule for examinations prior to Christmas 1890 was posted, it was quickly observed that the freshmen would complete their examinations at two o'clock on Monday and that the upper classes would not complete theirs until two o'clock on Wednesday. Someone had blundered. The schedule-maker did not know student psychology. A great howl went up. Something had to be done. There was no hope of moving the faculty to make a change. Some of the brighter student minds went to work with the following result:

While the freshmen were at supper on Sunday evening, a thoroughly organized band of upperclassmen went through the rooms of all freshmen, laid hold of their trunks and suitcases and carried them to wagons that were standing in readiness back of the old Chambers. The wagons were then driven several miles into the country and the trunks and suitcases were deposited in a farmer's lumber house and securely locked up. Only a few of the students ever knew where that farm was located. You can imagine the confusion that followed when the freshmen returned from supper and discovered that their luggage was gone. Some of them had already packed their suitcases in order to be ready for a speedy departure after examinations on Monday. One freshman came to my room to see if he could borrow a pistol. I never owned one in my life. Of course the freshmen did not get away on Monday nor yet on Tuesday. But on Wednesday sometime before noon a notice was posted on the bulletin board saying that the freshmen would find their trunks in the Infirmary rooms in the north end of Elm Row. The students who spirited the trunks away Sunday night had spirited them back in the wee hours of Tuesday night. So the freshmen and the upper classmen all went away on the same train Wednesday afternoon, and everybody was happy, or nearly everybody.

Mark Twain used to say that classical music is a great deal better than it sounds. Well, the Davidson students in those days were a great deal better than some of these incidents sound. A comparatively few students can do a lot of mischief. Not only so, but even good students can be swept off their feet by mob psychology, which is a very peculiar thing. Someone may say that I should not have recorded these incidents. I have to record them if I am going to write a story that is true to life. Besides, when I begin to say some good things about the students, I want the reader to know that I am not idealizing the life of those olden days, nor do I think those days were better than these. The Golden Age is not in the past. I am mindful of the words of the Preacher in Ecclesiastes: "Say not thou, What is the cause that the former days were better than these? for thou dost not enquire wisely concerning this."

As I turn back to the catalogue and recall each man, name by name, who was in college with me, I am convinced that the large majority of them deserved the praise bestowed upon them by the president in his report to the Trustees. The majority of them were mature young men (the average age being 22), and knew what they were here for. Many of them were from the country and had very little money and maybe less polish, but they meant business. Perhaps I can illustrate this by quoting a portion of a letter that was written in January, 1896. If I seem to use myself for illustrative purposes too often, please remember that I was requested to write my memories. In fact, I could not possibly write the memories of some other fellow. But let me get to the letter. In the winter of 1896 while I was in my senior year at Union Theological Seminary I received a call to the Presbyterian Church at Marion, Virginia. At the same time, I received an invitation to remain at the Seminary for two years as instructor in Greek and Hebrew. Being in a strait betwixt the two, I wrote Dr. J. M. Wharey, D.D., pastor of the church at Mooresville, North Carolina, for advice. He was chairman of the committee that had oversight of candidates for the ministry in Concord Presbytery and had been like a father to me, my own father having died ten years before.

In his reply, Dr. Wharey gave me some very helpful advice and then added: "Do you remember our first acquaintance when you stopped at my house on your way to college? When you left I said to Mrs. Wharey: 'There is something in that boy, he is going to make his mark in the world.' Now don't be too much uplifted but hear the reason I gave for the opinion. Not that I had perceived the touch of genius in your conversation or features, only both indicated fair abilities and determination to make the most of all opportunities, but I had observed a rent in your pants very neatly darned, and I continued to my wife: 'A boy that is not ashamed to wear patched breeches to college on his first entrance, and will study as I believe that boy will, is sure to make his mark.' "

Four Davidson Presidents

Left to Right:

Rev. John R. Cunningham, D.D., LL.D.
(1941-   )

Rev. Walter Lee Lingle, D.D., LL.D.
(1929-1941)

Prof. William J. Martin, Ph.D., M.D., LL.D.
(1912-1929)

Prof. Henry Louis Smith, Ph.D., LL.D.
(1901-1912)

L 9
DAVIDSON
COLLEGE

FOUNDED 1837 BY PRES-
BYTERIANS. NAMED FOR
GENERAL W. L. DAVIDSON.
WOODROW WILSON STUD-
IED HERE 1873-74.

Historic Campus Marker

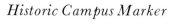

There were a good many boys with patched breeches in those days, and some with breeches that had not even been patched. They may not have been polished or brilliant, but they were dead in earnest, and were not given to smashing college property and college rules. It may be that some of them were lacking in a sense of humor and took things too seriously. At any rate they studied. Speaking of studying, it may be of interest to note the subjects that they studied. The courses in the freshman and sophomore years were very definitely prescribed. If students were candidates for the A.B. degree, and practically all of them were, their studies ran as follows: In the freshman year they took Latin, Greek, Math, Physics, and Biblical Instruction. In the sophomore year they took Latin, Greek, Math, Chemistry, English, and Biblical Instruction. The few who were candidates for the B.S. degree could substitute a modern language for Greek in the freshman year, and another modern language for Latin in the sophomore year.

In the junior year students for either A.B. or B.S. could select any five studies out of the following subjects: Latin, Greek, Math, Physics, Chemistry, English, History, French, German, and Biblical Instruction.

In the senior year students for either degree could select any five of the following subjects: Latin, Greek, Math, Applied Math, Astronomy and Meteorology, Geology and Mineralogy, Practical Chemistry, Logic and Political Economy, English, Mental and Moral Philosophy, and Bookkeeping and Commercial Law.

There you have the whole curriculum at that time. You will observe that it centered about Latin, Greek, Math, and Biblical Instruction. There were few if any elective courses. The passing grades were as follows: for freshmen 60, sophomores 65, juniors 70, and seniors 75. If the student made those grades he received his diploma. If he failed to make them there was no diploma for him.

We had not heard of majors, entrance units, semester hours, and quality points in those days. They were as remote as vitamins and electrons. The late John H. Finley, the brilliant editor of the New York *Times*, who was once a college president, made the following suggestion concerning the terms in which we measure education in these latter days:

> 50 minutes make an hour.
> 16 hours make a week.
> 16 weeks make a credit.
> 120 credits make a degree.

If there were too few courses in the curriculum in those early days, I am convinced that there are too many in these latter days. From time to time a college should re-define its objectives, and then re-adjust its curriculum in such a way as to point very definitely toward those objectives.

Perhaps we do not deserve too much credit for studying hard on those difficult subjects, if indeed we did, as there was not much else to do. There were no automobiles, no hitchhiking, no picture shows, no radios, no intercollegiate athletics, and no multiplicity of campus activities. We could not leave town without permission and could not leave the campus after seven in the evening. There were no cuts. In fact, such things had never been heard of. If a student was absent from class he had to give his excuse to the individual professor. If he considered the excuse valid, well and good. If not he gave the student a zero and the faculty gave him some demerits. A certain number of demerits meant expulsion from college. Those were hard and cruel days, but they got results.

However, there was a brighter side to life. There were a lot of attractive girls in town and a lot of hospitable homes. The statistics quoted above indicate that a large percentage of the students visited the town girls. There was a roller-skating rink on the second floor of a store downtown, and one on the first floor of Morrison Hall, the new Y.M.C.A. building. We had a wonderful time skating with the girls. We also played tennis with them and took them to church. I suppose the two things are associated in my mind because of an incident. As I left a visiting young lady at the door of her hostess after I had taken her to church one Sunday night, with a view to making an engagement, I said: "By the way, you play tennis, don't you?" She replied, "Not on the Sabbath." She never married.

We also enjoyed visiting in the homes of the professors and the hospitable homes of townspeople. I remember especially the home of Mrs. Holt who lived just across Main Street from Oak Row where I roomed. She lived alone after her young daughter, Julia, went off to college. She never left the premises during the years I was in college, and although I lived just across the street from her I never saw her in the front yard. In her earlier days she had been a teacher and was a cultured woman. In her after years she was a unique personality. There were quite a number of unique, not to say eccentric, personalities around town in those days. I enjoyed going to Mrs. Holt's. There was always a vacant chair in her sitting room and she left the impression that it had just been sitting there waiting for me. She was a kindly person and always had a good word to say of others. Although she was a recluse she knew more interesting news about the college and about the town than any other dozen people. She knew because her home was a regular mecca for students, and for townspeople too. Her kindly interest was always an inspiration to me. Bless her dear memory.

V ꝫ Extracurricular Activities

WHEN I BEGIN to sum them up, there appear to have been more extracurricular activities in those days than I had realized. Let us now glance at some of them.

We had no intercollegiate athletics, but plenty of intramural athletics of several types. Each class had a baseball team and there was considerable rivalry among the teams. My class won the championship in 1891. Somewhere in the Alumni Office there is a photograph of our class team. As I remember it, Dr. C. M. Richards was the best player in our class. We also had a good deal of tennis.

Intramural football interested me most. The fundamentals of the game were the same as they are now. The forward pass had not yet been introduced. A player could run on a fumbled ball if he was lucky enough to get it. There was no referee with a whistle to blow a signal to down the ball. The player who had the ball could crawl with it after he had been tackled, and the whole opposing team would pile on him until he cried, "Down!" If he did not have enough breath left in him to give that signal it was just too bad. With the flying-wedge and a number of other plays that have since disappeared, it was an even rougher game than it is today.

The *Davidson Monthly* carried a write-up of the 1890 Thanksgiving game that deserves a place in history and literature. Two captains were chosen. One was John Schenck, the uncle of Professor L. B. Schenck, and the other was Charles Robinson, the cousin of President W. J. Martin. Both the captains were a bit under size for heavy football, but both were as quick as a cat and made excellent backfield runners. They selected the players irrespective of class. Schenck selected me for the center (it was "center rush" in those days) of his team, and Robinson selected Charley Grey. Then they proceeded to alternate in selecting men until the teams were complete.

Here is the write-up in part: "The greatest thing in the world was the football game at Davidson College on last Thanksgiving. We cannot play Yale at New York or even Trinity [now Duke University] at Charlotte, but gentle friends, we can play Davidson College,

The Campus Well and Campus Vista

and so we did. If we could only get the faculty to think as we do we would gladly test our mettle on foreign foes, but they are mulish, so we have to play among ourselves. We had a good game, however, so one of the Trinity's alumni said who happened to be on the grounds. Such was the testimony of Dr. Martin [afterwards president of the college] who was one of the 'seven stone giants' at the University of Virginia last year, and ought to know a good game when he sees it.

"The field was hard fought, the score standing, when the game was called, 16 to 6 in favor of Captain Schenck. None of the players were killed or maimed for life, but honorable blood was shed, and it was with feelings of mutual respect that the two sides repaired at the close of the game to Scofield's and enjoyed a treat at the expense of the winning team. We had ladies to witness our struggles, and although they did not wear pink or blue stockings or lead around lap dogs bedecked with college colors, their hearts were in the right place, and they took a kindly interest in the players. We think our college could advertise herself in no way more successfully than to let us join the I.F.B.A., for we have a sneaking notion that we could clean something up if we only had a chance."

There you see amateur football as it was in those earlier days. It was the forerunner of organized, intercollegiate football, with coaches, referees, and all the latter-day trappings. The records show that the Davidson team played its first intercollegiate game in 1898, and that the first coach was employed in 1900. From that day to this, the Davidson football team has made an enviable record for itself and for the college, not simply for the victories won, but for playing "a fair game and a square game." The spirit of the team has been praised by spectators and sportswriters through all these years.

At times there has been a tendency on the part of a few over-zealous friends to push the Davidson team into big-time football, but such movements have never succeeded, and let us hope they never may. I have no objection to the college giving financial assistance to the student who is a football player if he needs it, but there is serious objection to scouring the country and hiring football players who do not naturally belong to our constituency. There is a great deal of difference between a group of college students who incidentally play football and a group of football players who incidentally go to college.

In addition to these organized games, students got exercise in roller skating and in ice skating when there was ice, in cross-country runs, in walking, and in chopping wood. They got a great deal of exercise in helping to build Lake Wiley. Week after week we repaired to the site of the dam, about a mile east of the college, and with pick, shovel, and wheelbarrow moved many tons of earth. We did it just for fun, too. The Federal Government never offered to pay us. What a shame! When the dam was completed, Dr. H. L. Smith, Superintendent of Buildings and Grounds, reported to the Trustees that he had ever so many picks, shovels, and wheelbarrows for sale, and hoped to realize a nice sum for them, to be put into the college treasury. When the lake was full it covered fourteen acres, and afforded lots of fun and exercise in swimming, boating, and tobogganing. The toboggan was a large sled on very small wheels. A track was laid on the steep hillside. The toboggan was placed on the track and filled with students. Sometimes young ladies were along. At a given signal the toboggan was released and scooted down that hill at a terrific speed, and out into the water, amid shrieks and yells. It was a pretty dangerous proposition, especially for those who could not swim. James M. Douglas, then a student, now professor of Physics, came near being drowned when he and W. W. Flowe went down the hill in the toboggan together and the toboggan sank.

Let us turn to the place religion occupied in our college life. In a Christian college religion should occupy first place. We had chapel, conducted by members of the faculty, every morning in the week. Some years it came before breakfast, and some years immediately after breakfast. At any rate it was at a very early hour, and sometimes students were seen running to chapel in various stages of dress, or undress. It was too early for one to be in a devotional frame of mind. I cannot remember that chapel made any definite impression upon me in one way or another. I have no doubt that it was good for me. However, I have always been strongly in favor of required chapel. Even apart from its religious values, it is the greatest single unifying influence in the college. It is the one time in the day when all the students are brought together in one body. I am sure that it can also be made of great spiritual value.

Speaking of chapel reminds me that one of the very few original pranks ever played by Davidson College students was in connection with a chapel service. It occurred long after my day. The scene was Shearer Hall, and the time was an early chapel service. The president and the professors who had notices to give sat on a long bench on the rostrum. Some genius wired the bench and connected the wires with the piano pedal in such a way that pressure on the pedal would close the electric circuit. The president gave out the hymn and sat down. The pianist struck up the tune. The first time he put his foot on the pedal, an electric current shot through the bench on which the president and his colleagues sat. They shot up like jack-out-of-the-box, to the great amazement of the students who did not know the cause. I have always wanted to know who that genius was. Someone has divided the people of the world into three classes: men, women, and college students.

We were required to attend church, too. Of course there were some protests from time to time in the *Davidson Monthly*. One generation of students has about as much human nature as another and sometimes more. But honestly, I did not find the requirement irksome. I had been required to go to church ever since I could remember and didn't know any better.

Rev. R. A. Webb was pastor of the church for a month or two after I entered college. In after years he became the effective teacher of Theology in the Louisville Presbyterian Seminary. He was a peculiar-looking little man in his early thirties when he was at Davidson. Even then there were indications that he was going to be a theologian. He had a class of seventeen college students studying the Presbyterian Confession of Faith, and they said they enjoyed it. After Dr. Webb left, Dr. Shearer supplied the church for several months.

Dr. Robert F. Campbell became the pastor in the spring of 1889, and remained until the summer of 1890. He left because of poor health. His friends did not think he would live long. He became pastor of the First Presbyterian Church of Asheville in 1892. In 1942 I helped to celebrate the fiftieth anniversary of his pastorate there. His bow still abides in strength in 1946 at the age of eighty-seven.

Rev. Alfred T. Graham became pastor of the Davidson church in 1891 and remained until 1907, when he became pastor of the Presbyterian Church at Lexington, Virginia. He meant a great deal to me personally, and I am sure that he did to many other students. From the above it will be seen that we had a succession of able and noble pastors while I was a student. But here is a strange thing. I attended church every Sunday morning and often on Sunday nights, but with one exception I cannot remember a single sermon any one of them ever preached or a single thing that one of them said from the pulpit. The one exception is a sermon that Dr. Campbell preached on the weather. People are always talking about the weather; why not preach about it? And I remember these helpful lines from the sermon:

> "If the weather is wet, do not fret;
> If the weather is dry, do not cry;
> If the weather is warm, do not storm;
> If the weather is cold, do not scold;
> But be thankful together,
> Whatever the weather."

When a Scots minister visited one of his members one Monday afternoon and discovered that she did not remember anything about the sermon on Sunday, he reminded her that a sermon would not do her any good if she could not remember it. She replied in her Scottish brogue which I will not try to reproduce: "I don't know about that. Do you see the clothes out there on the line? I put a great deal of water through them this morning. There is none in them now, but they are all the whiter for the water's having gone through them." Let us hope that the same was true of the sermons I heard.

But to show that I was not altogether hopeless, let me say that I remember with great distinctness the baccalaureate sermon which Dr. G. B. Strickler preached at the commencement of my sophomore year, of all times. His text was Psalm 119:18, and he preached a very impressive sermon. I had never heard of him before, but I learned to know him well in after years when he was professor of Theology in Union Theological Seminary, and heard him preach often. His sermons were always unforgettable. He had a way of putting them up in portable packages.

In 1935 by order of the Trustees, the long-standing custom requiring students to attend the regular Sunday morning church service was changed. Instead, a Sunday evening vesper service in the college chapel was substituted. Ministers who are believed to be especially qualified to speak to students are invited to conduct these services. Thus the students have the privilege of hearing a variety of ministers and messages during the year. The students' Glee Club, under the guidance of the Director of Music, leads the music for these services. Students are no longer required to attend the morning service at the church, but they are required to attend this vesper service in the college chapel, with a reasonable number of absences allowed. I trust that it is proper for me to express the hope that when the new church has been erected, this student vesper service may be transferred to the church, but that the general plan may remain much as it is. At the same time I trust that this church may be able to reach out and induce as many students as possible to attend the morning services of the church on a voluntary basis.

As I look back over the years I believe that the college Y.M.C.A. had more to do with the development of my spiritual life than the church. There was a devotional meeting by the students, of the students, and for the students one night each week. A student made the devotional talk, and there were hymns and prayers. For nearly two years I sat behind a post for fear the leader would see me and call on me to lead in prayer. And then they asked me to lead the meeting one night. That brought me out from behind the post, and

I tried to do my part from that time on. The Y.M.C.A. sent us out to teach mission Sunday schools and out on deputation work. After having a week's training under Dr. John R. Mott, they sent me in my senior and postgraduate years to visit many schools and colleges in North Carolina. All of that meant a great deal to me. From that day to this I have been a staunch believer in the college Y.M.C.A.

In the spring of my freshman year, Rev. P. Frank Price, who is now a veteran missionary but who had then just graduated from Union Theological Seminary, came to Davidson and preached for a week in the Presbyterian Church. He left a deep impression on me. During that week I met Dr. C. R. Harding on the street. With his inquiring mind, he said: "Mr. Price, how long do you expect to be here?" I replied that I would like to stay here three more years if they would let me. That is a trivial incident, but how could a freshman forget being mistaken for Dr. Price?

In the spring of my sophomore year, Dr. Robert E. Speer came to Davidson and spoke on foreign missions. He was then just a little over twenty-two years of age, and had only recently graduated from Princeton. I still think of that as the most impressive address I ever heard. As I have heard Dr. Speer again and again through the years, I believe all told he is the most impressive speaker I ever heard.

Speaking further of the religious life of the college, I note that the president of the college in his report to the Trustees in 1890 stated that there were 102 students in college, and that of these 89 were members of some evangelical church. Forty were candidates for the ministry. There were also quite a number of sons of ministers, but the number is not given.

Sometimes I think that it is a pity that anybody has to see candidates for the ministry in the making. They are just boys and some of them do things that candidates should not do, and some of them leave undone things that they should do, especially in their classroom work. But I have seen some very unpromising candidates grow into very useful ministers. Some people get the idea that candidates as a rule are mediocre, not to say dull. In looking over the list of valedictorians recently posted in the library, I observe that eight candidates for the ministry graduated at the head of their classes between 1918 and 1942. That was out of all proportion to the number of candidates in college.

Sons of ministers have also been much maligned. An incident will show how some otherwise intelligent people think of them. Along about 1932 a certain Captain Davidson of the United States Army had occasion to fly from Randolph Field in Texas to Washington from time to time. The airplane route from North to South goes right over Davidson College. Captain Davidson's attention was attracted by the large new Chambers Building. When upon inquiry he learned it was a part of Davidson College, he became interested. He liked the name Davidson. Accordingly, he wrote me that if we would have the name of Davidson College painted in large letters on the roof for the information of flying men, he would pay the bill. Duncan D. McBryde, of the class of 1933, and some of his colleagues painted the name in large letters on the roof on the east side of the building where it could not be seen from the ground. Captain Davidson sent me a check for forty dollars.

Then one summer day Captain Davidson stopped over to see the college that bore his name. As I showed him around I kept trying to put our best foot forward. Finally I began to tell him what wonderful students we had. Among other things I told him that we had sixty-five students who were sons of ministers. He exclaimed: "Oh, h---! That's terrible, isn't it?" I have never heard from Captain Davidson from that day to this. But the captain had a mistaken idea. In *Who's Who in America,* there is a larger percentage of sons of ministers than of men from any other calling. Right here at Davidson sons of ministers have made a distinguished record. Ten sons of ministers graduated at the head of their classes between 1918-1941. Woodrow Wilson, a Davidson student, was the son of a minister.

After all has been said about the religious influences and activities in the college, I suspect that the most potent religious influence was to be found in the daily lives of our professors in the classroom and on the campus. They were all fine Christian men. Their characters and personalities left a deep impression upon the students.

The place of personality in education might make a good theme for a thesis for some graduate student in the field of education.

In any adequate history of Davidson College, there should be a separate chapter on the two literary societies. The first session of the college began on March 12, 1837. In June of that same year the Eumanean and Philanthropic Literary Societies were organized. For three-quarters of a century they played a very large part in the lives of the students, and then interest began to subside. In my student days they were still going good and strong. Practically all students belonged to these societies. The questionnaire sent to the students by Dr. H. L. Smith in 1891 showed that over ninety-five per cent of the students were members. If a student did not join one or the other of the societies we wondered what was the matter with him.

The literary societies met twice a week. For many years the college had holiday on Saturday. During those years the societies met on Friday nights and Saturday mornings. In 1889 the weekly holiday was shifted from Saturday to Monday. The society meetings were then changed to Saturday nights and Monday mornings. In 1917 the weekly holiday was eliminated, and the college went on a six-day classroom schedule. That no doubt had much to do with the decreased interest in the societies.

The night meetings were devoted exclusively to debating. Subjects were chosen and members were assigned to the respective sides of the questions. The individual student had no choice as to which side of a question he would take. I have always had some sympathy with the stand Theodore Roosevelt took when a student at Harvard. He declined to debate on the side of a subject that he did not believe in. In the Philanthropic Society, to which I belonged, there were maximum and minimum limits as to the time a debater might speak. As I remember it, the minimum was three minutes and the maximum ten. The debater could not look at his watch, but if he transgressed either of these limits he was fined. The first time I debated I was fined fifty cents for speaking less than three minutes, and it seemed to me that I had been speaking for at least an hour. In our

Dormitory Row

debates we tackled some very difficult questions, especially along political and economic lines.

The morning meetings were given over to declamations by freshmen and sophomores, and original orations and essays by juniors and seniors. In all meetings there was an official critic who sat at a table on which there was a large dictionary. He criticized all performances with dignity and erudition. Sometimes his criticisms were unmerciful. After he was through the house was thrown open for criticisms, and there were always some voluntary critics.

Toward the close of the session there were spirited contests for the medals which were given to each department of the work. Freshmen and sophomores contested for the declaimer's medal, and juniors and seniors contested for the debater's and essayist's medals. Then each society chose its very best orators from the junior class to speak in a public exercise at commencement at a contest for the junior orator's medal. This was the most coveted prize in college. I spoke in one of those contests, but did not come in gunshot of the medal. I mention the fact only because my subject was "The Future of Constantinople." I took the ground that the Dardanelles should be and would be internationalized and opened up for the ships and commerce of all nations. That was more than fifty years ago, and my prophecy has not yet come true, but who knows but that it may come true in the near future.

It is a thousand pities that interest in the societies has decreased. There were many causes for this. Student life is crowded with many other activities. Classroom work now occupies six days a week, leaving very little room for the societies. The student body has grown too large for two societies. Fraternities have absorbed an increasing amount of the time and thought of many students. Of course the societies are still carrying on, and all honor to those students who have stood by them through thick and thin. But it would mean much to the students and much to the college if there could be a revival of interest in the societies and if they could play as large a part in student life as they did in their best days.

There was no organized student government in college when I was a student. That did not come until about 1910. But there was always student honor and, in a sense, student government. In my day cheating on examination or on any pledged work was the one unpardonable sin. If a student was discovered cheating, and he knew that he was discovered, he did not wait for trial. He packed his trunk and left immediately. On one examination after my time, a student who realized that he had been discovered cheating went to his room and took his own life. So deep was the shame connected with cheating. In an oratorical contest in one of the societies a student delivered for an original oration, John Temple Graves' Eulogy on Henry Grady. When his plagiarism was discovered he did not tarry, but left college immediately.

Although there was no organized student government, students sometimes acted. In my senior year it was discovered that two students, one a senior, had a five-gallon keg of whisky in their room, and were selling it to any who wanted to buy. The senior class met and ordered the two students to leave college within twenty-four hours. Feeling that the senior class had no legal authority to send them away, one of the students is said to have appealed to the president of the college, who, after hearing his story, told him that he was getting off mighty light, as his performance might have landed him in the penitentiary. To this day student government and student honor constitute one of the very finest things about Davidson College.

There were only three fraternities at Davidson in 1888: Kappa Alpha, Sigma Alpha Epsilon, and The Mystic Seven, which was merged into Beta Theta Pi in 1889. The Kappa Sigma chapter was organized in 1890. These fraternities had their halls in the Old Chambers Building. At each end of Chambers on each floor, there was a dormitory for a single student. Each fraternity was located at the end of Old Chambers, and had the single room and the double room next to it. Less than half of the students belonged to these fraternities. As the student body was comparatively small, that means that the fraternities did not have over twelve or fifteen members each. In this small group the student made some very intimate friends. Fraternities are not democratic institutions, and yet I do not think that the fraternities were very snobbish. So far as my observation went they never got very deep into college politics. I do not remember ever having heard anything that savored of politics mentioned at any meeting of the fraternity to which I belonged. There were no large initiation fees in those early days and no big social functions that called for money. If my memory serves, my fraternity did not cost me over ten dollars a year. It could not possibly have cost me any more than that for I did not have it.

As the student body grew and the number of fraternities increased, it was found to be more and more undesirable to have the fraternity halls in Old Chambers. There was much talk of building chapter houses. The matter was up rather frequently, not only in fraternity plans and discussions, but in the meetings of the faculty and of the Trustees. While those discussions were going on the fraternities were moved from Old Chambers, in 1917, to Oak Row, Elm Row, and the first floors of the Eumanean and Philanthropic Society halls. There they remained for nine years. This arrangement grew more and more unsatisfactory. In 1926 the fraternities moved out into residences which they bought or rented in various parts of the town. It was soon apparent that this was not going to be satisfactory to students, faculty, or Trustees. It took away from the dormitories many fine students whose influence was needed on the campus. Not only so, but it made fraternities less democratic than they had been before. Besides, the old residences, which were rented or bought, were not suitable as dormitories for students. The problem was solved when the college built the present Fraternity Court, in 1928. National secretaries of fraternities who have visited Davidson seem to be almost unanimous in the opinion that we have the best solution to the housing problem of fraternities for a small college that they have found in the many colleges which they have visited.

It will be seen from this sketch of our activities that we did not lead drab lives that were occupied exclusively with thoughts of the binomial theorem, Greek and Latin roots, or the fine distinctions of the aorist and subjunctive in Greek. On the contrary we lived very happy and wholesome lives. Those days will always be among the very brightest in our memories.

VI 🙚 The Intervening Years

My CLASS GRADUATED from Davidson in 1892. I returned to the college the next session to take postgraduate work in English under Dr. W. S. Currell. So it was in May, 1893, that I said farewell to my college days. In 1903 I attended my first meeting of the Trustees. During the ten intervening years I kept in rather close touch with the college. The fact that Miss Merle Dupuy, of Davidson, and I were married on January 2, 1900, will explain why I had occasion to make frequent visits to Davidson before and after that date.

There were many changes in the college during those ten intervening years. It is the aim of this chapter to make mention of some of those changes as gleaned from memory and from the records.

The most marked changes were in the faculty. During the five years I was a student there was not a single change in the faculty. After that, changes came swiftly. Professor W. S. Graves resigned the chair of Latin and French and left in the summer of 1893. Dr. W. S. Currell, professor of English, left Davidson for Washington and Lee University in 1895. Colonel W. J. Martin, the veteran professor of Chemistry, died on March 23, 1896. Dr. W. D. Vinson, professor of Mathematics, died suddenly on August 20, 1897. That list includes three of the best teachers I ever knew. Some of us felt that Davidson would never be the same again. We had not learned the lesson that John Wesley tried to impress upon his followers. As he neared the end of his life, his followers were quite sure that his death would be the end of the Methodist movement. He answered them by saying that the workers may die, but the Lord's work goes on. That truth has been illustrated many times in the history of Davidson College.

Inasmuch as the successors of these men and other professors who were elected during the next ten or twelve years became the backbone of the college for thirty-five or forty years, they deserve more than passing mention. Dr. W. R. Grey became professor of Latin and French in 1893 and continued to fill that position in a scholarly manner until his retirement in 1934. Dr. Thomas P. Harrison was elected professor of English in 1895 and held that position

South Court and South Wing of Chambers

until 1908 when he accepted the chair of English in the North Carolina College of Agriculture and Engineering, Raleigh, North
Carolina.

Dr. W. J. Martin, Jr., was elected professor of Chemistry in 1896,
and filled that chair with distinction until his election as president
of the college in 1912. Dr. John L. Douglas became professor of
Mathematics in 1897 and served in that position with ability until
his retirement in 1935. His death occurred on January 5, 1937.

The most marked change in the faculty during the ten intervening years was brought about by the resignation of President J. B.
Shearer and the election of Dr. Henry Louis Smith as president in
1901. Dr. Smith had been vice-president since 1897, and had performed many of the duties of the president. It is interesting to note
in Dr. Shearer's resignation that he did not hesitate to tell the Trustees that he thought Dr. Smith should be elected president. The
Trustees might think it a little presumptuous today if a retiring
president were to nominate his successor. It was very natural in
Dr. Shearer's case, for he and the Trustees had already seen Dr.
Smith in action as vice-president. The Trustees elected Dr. Shearer
vice-president, and requested him to continue as professor of Biblical
Instruction. He filled these two positions until his death on June
14, 1919.

Dr. Smith's duties as president made it necessary for him to re-
linquish his work as professor of Physics. Dr. J. M. Douglas became
assistant professor of Physics in 1901, and was made full professor
of that department in 1903. He filled that position with great satisfaction until his retirement in 1944.

Because of advancing age, Dr. Shearer asked for an assistant in
his department. In response to that request, Dr. M. E. Sentelle was
elected associate professor of Biblical Instruction in 1904. Three
years later he was elected full professor of Philosophy, and was
known by that title in the catalogue until after the death of Dr.
Shearer. However, he continued to teach courses in the English
Bible. From 1920 until his retirement in 1944, he was known as the
"J. W. Cannon Professor of Bible and Philosophy." He was elected
Dean of Students in 1920 and continued as dean until 1941 when

he asked to be relieved. As dean he probably did as much to uphold the moral and academic standards of the college as any man ever connected with it.

Dr. J. M. McConnell was elected associate professor of Latin and Mathematics in 1904. In 1907 he was elected professor of History and Economics. Later he was relieved of the courses in Economics and gave his full time to History. By the revision of the Constitution and By-Laws of the Trustees in 1928 the office of Dean of Instruction was created. The name was later changed to Dean of the Faculty. Dr. McConnell was promptly elected to fill this office. As professor and dean and by his own personality he exercised a very large influence for good upon the college up to the time of his sudden death on May 16, 1935.

Professor Archibald Currie, after having served as Instructor and Librarian for a number of years, was elected associate professor of Latin and Mathematics in 1906. He was elected full professor of Elementary Law, Education, and Public Speaking in 1913. Later he was made the Woodrow Wilson Professor of Economics and Political Science. This position he filled with distinction until his death on December 30, 1942.

In 1907 Dr. J. W. MacConnell was elected professor of Physical Training and Biology. At the same time he was elected College Physician. He was inaugurated as professor at the commencement of 1908. Later his title was changed to professor of Physiology and Hygiene. He also served as College Physician until his retirement in 1945. In these several positions he rendered a large service to Davidson College.

Those who know anything about the history of Davidson College know that the men whose names are mentioned above were a tower of strength to Davidson College for many years. As they, too, have passed to their reward or have retired, we again feel that the college will never be quite the same without them. Again we need to remember the saying of John Wesley: "The workers may die, but the Lord's work goes on."

There were also some marked changes in the grounds and buildings during the intervening years. Soon after the death of Colonel

W. J. Martin in 1896, alumni and friends began a movement to raise funds for the erection of a science building as a memorial to him. This building was completed and opened for service on March 6, 1901. It was named "The Martin Chemical Laboratory." The cost of the building was approximately ten thousand dollars, but as dollars went further in those days than now, it was a much better building than the cost would indicate. It was a long step in advance of anything that Davidson ever had before. It was located about four feet west of where the Hugh A. and Jane Parks Grey Memorial Library now stands. There it stood and served the college for thirty-nine years. It was removed in 1940 to make way for the Library. However, it was replaced by a handsome science building in 1941, to be known as "The Martin Science Building" in honor of the father, Colonel W. J. Martin, virtual founder of the department of Chemistry, and of his son, Dr. W. J. Martin, Jr., who served as professor of Chemistry for seventeen years, and after that as president of the college for seventeen years.

The Old Chapel was transformed into Shearer Biblical Hall during the intervening years. The change was effected during 1901 and the building was formally turned over to the president of the college on February 13, 1902. The minutes of the Trustees indicate that the cost of this transformation was approximately seven thousand dollars, which was contributed by Dr. Shearer.

In the *Davidson College Magazine* of May, 1901, there is an article by Dr. Henry Louis Smith describing the changes that were made in the Old Chapel in order to transform it into Shearer Hall. Perhaps a paragraph or two from that article will be of interest.

"Part of the walls of the Old Chapel, which was erected in 1837, will be utilized in the new building. The present entrance, facing the south, will be taken away, and a handsome portico be built on the west, thus making the new hall face the main street of the village. An addition will be placed on the east side of the present Chapel, running back 33 feet toward the Y.M.C.A. building (Morrison Hall). The whole upper floor, seating about 550, or more, will be used as a hall for morning prayers, and for all minor college celebrations, lectures, oratorical contests, etc. . . . The first floor will be divided into five rooms: two large classrooms, one for the Professor of Bible; a spacious college reading room, and commodious offices for the President and his secretary. The whole building will be heated and ventilated by furnaces placed in the basement under the northeast corner . . . The exterior is to be finished in stucco, and will present a handsome appearance from almost any part of the town. It will fill a pressing need, and bear witness for generations to come to the wise and thoughtful generosity of the donor."

It no doubt did fill a pressing need and served the college well until the New Chambers Building was erected in the latter nineteen-twenties. But now there are some of us who wish that it could be restored to the Old Chapel as we knew it back in the gay nineties. In fact, we hear with joy that there is a movement on foot to restore not only the Old Chapel, but the original quadrangle, and make of it the art and music center of the college. Such a movement will have the good wishes of many.

Another change on the campus was the removal of Old Tammany. That was a two-story building located on the east side of the original quadrangle, between Phi Hall and Elm Row. It was erected in 1837 as a residence for one of the professors. In my student days it was used as a dormitory for students. It was removed while the Old Chapel was being transformed into Shearer Hall, and a part of the Old Tammany material was used in that reconstruction.

Along this line a paragraph from the report of President Henry Louis Smith to the Trustees in May, 1902, is interesting. It reads thus: "The removal of Tammany has very much improved the appearance of the Campus. It is hoped that Oak Row and Elm Row may in the near future share the same fate." This is not the only reference to the proposed removal of those ancient landmarks. The rapid growth of the student body under the energetic administration of President Henry Louis Smith saved them. They were needed for dormitories. In the president's report to the Trustees in May, 1906, this paragraph occurs: "For many years, the College has been removing one after another the old buildings erected in 1837 on the original College Quadrangle. It has been the intention of the College authorities, should our College dormitory accommodations be sufficient without them, to remove Oak Row and Elm Row also, but the rapidly increasing number of students has thus far made it necessary to retain them. If, however, at any time our dormitory accommodations should be sufficiently increased to render their use unnecessary, these two buildings will be promptly removed, as they mar, to a great extent, the beauty of the Campus."

I was a member of the Trustees when that paragraph was read. So far as I can recall no one opposed the removal of these old landmarks. Nor do I recall that I felt any rising tide of opposition in my own heart. But something has evidently happened to me. When we were planning a new building program prior to the Centennial in 1937, and an architect suggested that those two buildings should be removed, and that perhaps along with them Shearer Hall and the two Literary Society Halls should go, I felt a violent protest deep down in my heart, and expressed it in no uncertain terms.

In 1902 a new dormitory was erected at a cost of approximately thirteen thousand dollars. The Trustees in 1906 voted to name it "The Rumple Dormitory," in honor of Dr. Jethro Rumple of Salisbury, North Carolina, who was a trustee of the College from 1878 to his death in 1906, and secretary of the Trustees from 1878 to 1905.

An event of first-class importance took place during the college year 1898-99. Water works were installed by the college. Prior to that time, as described in a previous chapter, students secured water for all purposes by drawing it from two wells, one located near Phi Hall and the other in the hallway of the Old Chambers Building. An epidemic of typhoid in the summer of 1898 made it necessary to abandon the wells and to construct a water system. A paragraph or two from the minutes of the Trustees will describe the process by which this was done. "Several wells were bored to an average depth of one hundred feet for a temporary supply. Then an attempt was made to sink an artesian well through the granite stratum. After going down five hundred feet, and not securing an adequate supply of water, this well was abandoned, and six wells were sunk in a group, that were flowing wells, furnishing about one hundred thousand gallons of pure water every twenty-four hours. Plans are made to have this water conveyed to a suitable reservoir, and the supply will be abundant." In the report of Dr. Henry Louis Smith, who was Superintendent of Grounds and Buildings, to the Trustees in May, 1900, we read: "The water works have proved satisfactory. The quantity of water is quite remarkable, and the supply so abundant that the engine runs only about two hours a day, to supply the whole College and all the families and boarding houses that use the system." The system was installed and supervised by Dr. Smith as Superintendent of Grounds and Buildings.

After this adequate supply of water was secured, another event of first-rate importance followed upon its heels. The first shower bath, or bath of any kind, in the history of the college was installed. It was placed in the little one-story room attached to the east side of Morrison Hall. You will recall that the first floor of that hall was used as a gymnasium. A little coal stove and a water tank were placed in one end of that little room, and the shower in the other end. Mr. F. L. Jackson, who was a student at that time, says that the only sure way for a student to get a shower was to build a fire in that little stove, and then stand guard until the water was warm lest some other student should come in and, wittingly or unwittingly, get the water that he was heating for himself. A year or two later, when Rumple Dormitory was erected, showers were installed there, and Davidson College was on the way. In 1924 when the town of Davidson installed an adequate water system, the college discarded its own system, and has since purchased its water from the town. As previously stated, the college now uses about one hundred gallons of water a day for each student. It has been said that the culture and civilization of any people or nation can be judged by the amount of soap and water used. Davidson should rate high at present. Perhaps we are trying to make up for the water that the college did not use between 1837 and 1900.

Another long step in advance was taken when the Trustees authorized the president of the college "to put in a complete electric light system for the College grounds and buildings, when he could raise the money for the purpose." Within a year he had raised the money and installed the system. Kerosene lamps were put out of commission. When the Duke Power Company (then known as the Southern Power Company) ran its high power lines across Davidson College lands in 1908, the little dynamo was supplanted, and from that day to this the college has been using current generated by the Duke Power Company. The increased use of electric current from year to year, as reflected in the reports of the treasurer of the college, makes an interesting study. The increase has been caused by the erection of new buildings and by better lights in the buildings and on the campus, and by the use of radios and other electrical appliances.

One of the most marked changes during the years that intervened between 1893 and 1903 was the rapid development in the field of Athletics and Physical Training. The Davidson College Athletic Association was organized in the fall of 1893. The first Athletic Day was observed in the spring of 1894. After that it became an annual feature. The first intercollegiate football game was played in Charlotte with the University of North Carolina on November 5, 1898. The score stood, University of North Carolina 11, Davidson 0. It was considered a "moral victory," as Carolina had a highly trained team. The second intercollegiate game was played in Charlotte with the University of South Carolina on Thanksgiving, 1898. The score was Davidson 6, South Carolina 0.

Dr. W. J. Martin, Jr., the new professor of Chemistry, who had been on the University of Virginia team, helped to coach the Davidson team for those two games. In the *Davidson College Magazine* for October, 1898, we find this interesting item: "Messrs. Stevens and Schenck (John R. Schenck of the class of '93) are to coach the team for the season's work, and will probably get them licked into shape in a short while. Mr. Stevens is the University of North Carolina's famous halfback, and undoubtedly the best halfback the South has ever produced. Mr. Schenck is an old Davidson man and is reputed to be the best quarterback the College ever had."

President Shearer felt that it was necessary to explain the whys and wherefores of this new departure to the Trustees. So in his report to the commencement meeting of the Trustees in 1899 we find this paragraph: "In response to the continued importunity of the students the faculty conceded to them the permission to engage in intercollegiate athletics, to the extent of playing two games of football away from Davidson, under the oversight and control of a member of the Faculty. This was granted as an experiment, without any promise as to the future. These games were played in due course, and everything passed off in a safe and satisfactory manner. This being a departure from previous usage, we properly report to the Board."

In response to the above the Trustees very properly took this action: "That the matter of College Athletics be referred to the faculty, with authority to deal with the whole matter with such care and discretion as shall not, on the one hand, discourage the young men, nor on the other lead to dissipation." From that day to this Davidson has continued to engage in intercollegiate athletics.

In December, 1899, the *Davidson College Magazine* carried this editorial: "In the name of the Athletic Association and the entire student body we wish to extend our thanks to Mr. R. S. Cromartie, of the Senior class of the Medical College, for his faithful and efficient work on the football team. At a sacrifice of much valuable time, he has spent every afternoon on the football field, and his long experience and careful training have made his coaching invaluable, while his steady work in the line has made it one of the strongest teams in the South." Mr. Cromartie graduated from Davidson in 1895. During his four years in college he was an outstanding football player. In the fall of 1899 we find him coaching the team and at the same time playing on it. The rules of eligibility were not so strict in those days. However, it should be said that as a student in the old Medical College, he was taking some courses in science in Davidson College, and his name is listed in the College catalogue for 1899-1900 as a student.

In the December, 1899, issue of the *Davidson College Magazine,* regret is expressed that whisky had appeared at the intercollegiate games. From that day to this whisky has been a curse at many football games throughout the country. It should be said in all fairness that the use of whisky has been reduced to a minimum for many years at the games played in the Davidson stadium.

In the catalogue of 1901-1902, the name of Mr. John A. Brewin appears as "Physical Director." In President Smith's report to the Trustees at the commencement meeting of 1902 this paragraph occurs: "Never before have the students enjoyed such opportunities of physical training as during the past year . . . The gymnasium classes have been maintained with zeal and persistence, and the records of the football and baseball teams in the field of intercollegiate athletics have been an almost unbroken series of victories . . . The Physical Director, Mr. John A. Brewin, has proved zealous, popular and efficient." It was a part of Mr. Brewin's duties to coach the football and baseball teams. He was Davidson's first full-time Physical Director and Coach. He remained at Davidson only two or three years. Thus we see the beginnings of Davidson's larger program of athletics and physical education.

During the years that intervened between 1893 and 1903, caps and gowns were introduced as proper dress for seniors at commencement, and on other public occasions. There is a delightful editorial on the subject in the *Davidson College Magazine* for November, 1897. It was written by the gifted editor, Mr. W. G. Perry of the class of 1898, who, by the way, wrote the best editorials we have ever seen in a Davidson student publication. The class of 1898 voted unanimously for caps and gowns, but the faculty voted just as unanimously against them. The class of 1901 made another attempt to secure caps and gowns, and again there is a delightful editorial in the magazine for September, 1900, from the pen of Mr. Reed Smith, another gifted editor. Again the faculty vetoed the request.

The class of 1903 took a different approach and presented their request to the Executive Committee of the Trustees. In the report of the Executive Committee to the Trustees at their commencement meeting, 1903, we find this paragraph: "The Senior class, wishing to use the academic Caps and Gowns upon public occasions, the matter was presented to your Committee, which answered that they saw nothing improper in the matter, and so gave consent to their use." Then the Trustees as a whole adopted this recommendation of a special committee: "We recommend the approval of the action of the Executive Committee with reference to the Senior Caps and

Gowns." That resolution was adopted at my first meeting with the Trustees. All that sounds amusing now, but it was serious enough then. At any rate, there you have the beginning of the modern academic procession at Davidson.

During these intervening years, the president of the college got an office of his own on the campus, and a private secretary, for the first time in the history of the college, so far as we can discover. Dr. Shearer had his office in his home, which was located across Main Street from the Old Chapel (Shearer Hall). He wrote all his letters with his own pen. He did not seem to have a letter file, but kept his letters in neat little bundles on his desk, or stowed away in his desk drawers. By the way, the residence he occupied had to be removed in 1931, as it was about to fall down, owing to the inferiority of the brick with which it was built. The brick was used to build a walk on the west side of the campus, parallel with Main Street and running from the northern edge of the campus to the church. As Rev. J. Blanton Belk looked on he remarked that he was sure that if the house had to be removed, Dr. Shearer would rejoice to know that the bricks were used to build a walk to the house of the Lord.

President Smith's new office was located in the newly reconstructed Shearer Hall, and Richard T. Gillespie, a student, who afterwards became president of Columbia Theological Seminary, was his secretary. With an office, a secretary who knew stenography and typing, a typewriter, letter files and such other appliances as had been invented at that time, the new president launched out upon a new era in the history of Davidson College.

The first issue of *Quips and Cranks,* the college annual, was published in 1895. Quite a number of its thirteen editors became distinguished men in after years. It is a modest-looking volume compared with the sumptuous editions published between 1930 and 1942. However, it contains much valuable historical material. It was dedicated in a very gracious way to President John Bunyan Shearer. The students would have been surprised if they had seen a paragraph in the report which President Shearer made to the Trustees in June, 1895. It reads thus: "The students of the College are publishing an annual this year. They wish the Executive Committee to subscribe for twenty-four copies at $1.50 each, to be sent as advertisements of the College to Libraries, Y.M.C.A. Rooms, and so forth. The Faculty agreed to endorse this request. Since this endorsement was made, the book has appeared, and contains some very objectionable matter, which the Faculty certainly would not have endorsed." It is needless to say that the Executive Committee did not take the twenty-four copies.

I have looked over that first volume to see if I can discover the objectionable matter. There is certainly nothing risque in it. Every bit of it could be published in the *Sunday School Times*. There are some clever take-offs of the members of the faculty, and some humorous touches about the college. I have always wondered whether Dr. Shearer had a sense of humor, notwithstanding the fact that he told many jokes, both new and old, in his classroom.

The Otts Lectureship was founded during the intervening years. On June 7, 1894, Rev. John M. P. Otts, D.D., L.L.D., of Greensboro, Alabama, began the foundation for this lectureship by giving the college the sum of $2,500. By other contributions and by additions from some of the interest earned from this investment the fund has grown to the sum of $10,000. The purposes of the lectureship and the conditions under which it was endowed are clearly and fully stated in two pages of the minutes of the Trustees of the date June 12, 1894.

By way of illustrating what he had in mind, Dr. Otts delivered a series of lectures at Davidson in the spring of 1893 which are printed in a book with the title, *Unsettled Questions*. I had the privilege of hearing these lectures, and they are probably the most helpful lectures ever delivered in connection with the Otts Foundation.

The next series of lectures on this foundation was delivered in the fall of 1897 by Dr. Robert L. Dabney, who was a professor in Union Theological Seminary for many years, and who wrote a profound book known as Dabney's Theology. He was one of the very greatest theologians our Church has produced, if not the greatest. When he came to deliver the Otts Lectures he was advanced in years and totally blind, and yet his mind seemed to be perfectly clear. With his white hair and beard he looked like a venerable patriarch or prophet. He chose for his subject, "Christ Our Penal Substitute." When he selected that as his subject he must have forgotten that he was ever a college student. At least he must not have known the mind of college students in 1897.

The *Davidson College Magazine* for December, 1897, carried a very illuminating editorial on the subject by W. G. Perry, the editor, who afterwards became professor of English in Georgia Tech. Here are a few excerpts from the editorial: "The choice of the subject of the course, we fear, was an unfortunate one; not in itself, but as delivered at Davidson. The topic would have been one that would have been interesting and instructive to the upper classes of a theological seminary . . . Starting with premises of which we know nothing they wound through abstract and intricate courses of reasoning, combating heresies of which we had never heard, establishing principles equally unknown, and reached a conclusion that left us—possibly a little more dazed than the premises.

"The College men had looked forward to hearing this grand, warworn soldier of Christ as toward a rare intellectual feast, and turned out en masse to hear the first lecture; but after vainly wrestling with the distinctions of 'Actual Guilt,' 'Potential Guilt,' and 'Sinfulness,' the temperature of their ardor dropped several degrees . . . We understand that these lectures are the result of an endowment, and suppose that the idea behind the endowment was benefit to the college student. Let us beg that in the future milk be given to the babes and meat saved for the strong men."

I have referred to these lectures by Dr. Dabney, not as a criticism of the great man. His greatness is so well established that no criticism could make even a dent in his reputation. But I refer to them to illustrate how even a great man may miss the purpose for which this lectureship was established. As a matter of fact, very few of the lecturers on this foundation during the fifty years since it was endowed have gotten down to where college students live. It might be a fine thing if Mr. Perry's respectful and illuminating editorial could be printed in full and sent to each lecturer the moment he accepts the invitation to deliver the Otts Lectures.

The mention of Dr. Dabney's name brings to mind a very interesting day I had with him on the Davidson campus during his visit here. At that time I was a young instructor of Hebrew and Greek in Union Theological Seminary, but was back at Davidson on one of those visits to which I referred in the opening paragraph of this chapter. One morning a note came from Dr. Shearer requesting me to take Dr. Dabney over to the campus and show him the college. I had seen Dr. Dabney but had never met him. He was seventy-seven years of age, totally blind, wore a white beard, and looked like my childish conceptions of the Old Testament patriarchs and prophets. He was regarded as perhaps the most profound theological thinker in our Church at that time. I naturally stood in awe of a great man like that.

But how could I show a blind man the college? That was the question that perplexed me. He quickly solved that problem by asking me to take him to the axis of the campus and turn his face toward the main building. I took him to a point on the walk near Phi Hall and turned his face toward the Old Chambers Building. Then he asked me to tell him in detail all that I saw in front of us. After that he asked me to describe what I saw on our right hand and on our left. He asked for a minute description and history of every building. He fired questions at me like a machine gun.

When he had finished seeing Davidson College he began firing questions at me about Union Theological Seminary, then located at Hampden-Sydney, where he had been professor from 1853 to 1883. When he was through I felt like a squeezed lemon. By this barrage of questions he had extracted from me all that I knew about Davidson College and Union Theological Seminary. It was a great day in the experience of a young minister.

It will be seen from this sketch that many changes took place in the college during the ten years that elapsed between the time I left Davidson as a student and returned as a trustee. In fact, there were more changes than the college had seen in any ten years of its previous history. The college was getting ready during those closing years of the nineteenth century to launch out upon a new and greater era in the twentieth.

VII 🍂 With the Trustees

NEARLY SIX HUNDRED different men have served as trustees of Davidson College since it was founded in 1837. Some of them served only a few years. Several have served for fifty years or more. Davidson owes a large debt of gratitude to these trustees who have given much of their time and often of their money to the college. Prior to 1914, trustees paid their own traveling expenses to the meetings of the Board, unless the presbyteries which elected them were thoughtful enough to take care of expenses, and that does not seem to have occurred very often. Since 1914, the traveling expenses of the trustees have been paid out of the college budget. My hat is off to the long line of noble men who have served Davidson College so faithfully as trustees. Among them have been some of the greatest men our Church has produced.

As stated in a previous chapter, I attended my first meeting of the Trustees at the commencement meeting in 1903. It was a venerable-looking body to me. Perhaps it would not look so venerable to me since I have grown older. I stood in much awe of some of them. I had not had the experience of my friend and fellow trustee, Mr. R. A. Dunn, which removed his awe. He became a trustee in 1893 while he was still a very young man. In those horse and buggy days, the trustees spent several days at Davidson during the commencement meeting. At one of those meetings, Mr. Dunn, the young layman, was put in the same room with two or three venerable Doctors of Divinity. Room was at a premium on commencement occasions. The young trustee was struck dumb with awe in the presence of these fathers of the Church. But the next morning when he awoke and saw two or three of these venerable fathers pottering around the room in their bare feet and in long, flowing nightshirts, looking for their razors and fresh linen, his awe forsook him. He still had great respect for them, but his awe was gone.

Let me mention a few of the trustees whom I saw at my first meeting. Rev. W. J. McKay, D.D., was president of the Trustees. He was the father of Drs. Robert and Hamilton McKay, of Charlotte. Dr. McKay graduated from Davidson in 1870 and served as a trustee from 1874 until his death in 1920. From 1893 to 1905, he was president of the Trustees. After that, he was secretary of the Trustees from 1906 until his death on December 10, 1920. Altogether he was a trustee for forty-six years. For a large part of that time, he was on the Executive Committee. No trustee ever served the college with greater devotion. I always think of him as a man of rare common sense.

In 1903, Rev. Jethro Rumple, D.D., of Salisbury, North Carolina, was secretary of the Trustees, a position which he filled from 1878 to 1905. He graduated from Davidson in 1850 and was a trustee of the college from 1858 until his death on January 20, 1906, a total of forty-eight years. He was a member of the Executive Committee from 1872 to 1906. Dr. Rumple was a large, impressive-looking man. He was regarded as one of the most scholarly men in the Synod of North Carolina. I like to think of him in connection with an incident related by Mrs. Hope Summerell Chamberlain in her book, *This Was Home.*

When she was a small girl she went to the manse in Salisbury to recite the Shorter Catechism to Dr. Rumple, her pastor. She got along finely until she was about halfway through and there she stalled on a word that she could not recall. Dr. Rumple told her to go out into the flower garden and look at the flowers for a while and the word would come to her, but it just would not come. When he called her in, he picked up the Catechism just where they left off and read the answer up to and including the word she stalled on, and without cracking a smile said, "This is where we left off." She took it up there and went through with flying colors. She never knew whether he purposely or inadvertently repeated the word she could not recall, but she liked to think he did it purposely, and so do I.

Mr. George E. Wilson, of Charlotte, was attorney for the Trustees in 1903. He was the father of Mr. George E. Wilson, Jr., who is now postmaster in Charlotte. Mr. Wilson was a trustee and a member of the Executive Committee from 1888 to his death in 1920. He was a member of the class of 1867, and after leaving Davidson, graduated in law from the University of Virginia. In

Charlotte, he was a lawyer, president of a bank, and an elder in the First Presbyterian Church. He took his work as trustee very seriously and served the college with the utmost devotion.

Dr. E. Nye Hutchison, a physician and an elder in the First Presbyterian Church of Charlotte, was the most venerable member of the Board in 1903. He was a member of the class of 1845, and served as a trustee from 1854 until his death in 1908, a total of fifty-four years. That is the longest term of service of any trustee in the history of Davidson College. Mr. R. A. Dunn, another elder in the First Presbyterian Church of Charlotte, came next in length of service. He was a trustee for fifty-two years. Dr. Hutchison was secretary of the Trustees from 1855 to 1878.

Some years ago while I was in the study of Rev. Stuart Nye Hutchison, D.D., pastor of East Liberty Presbyterian Church, Pittsburgh, and one-time Moderator of the General Assembly of the Presbyterian Church, U.S.A., I observed a Davidson College commencement program of 1845, neatly framed and hanging on the wall. He had an extra copy which he gave me, and I brought it to the Davidson College Library. On the program are the names of Dr. Stuart Nye Hutchison's father, Sylvanus Nye Hutchison, valedictorian of the class, who afterwards became a distinguished minister and a trustee of Davidson College; E. Nye Hutchison, salutatorian of the class, who became a physician and an active elder in the Presbyterian Church, as well as a trustee of the college; and my uncle Moses Lingle, one of the commencement orators, who became a teacher and farmer and an active elder in the Presbyterian Church for many years. Somehow that program has made me admire the Hutchisons even more than I did before.

My most vivid memory of Dr. E. Nye Hutchison is in connection with the Union Seminary Board, of which he was also a member for years. In my student days at the Seminary it was still the custom of the Board to send a committee of its members to the Seminary during the final examinations to hear the professors give their students oral examinations on everything they had been over during the session. One year Dr. E. Nye Hutchison, the physician and layman, was a member of that examining committee. He seemed to

Y.M.C.A. and Guest House

get along pretty well until he struck the examination of our class in Hebrew which was conducted by Dr. Walter W. Moore. As Dr. Moore was a native of Charlotte and had been brought up in the First Presbyterian Church of that city, it was incumbent upon Dr. Hutchison, an elder in that church, to be wide-awake and on the alert as Dr. Moore skillfully conducted that examination, even if it was in Hebrew. For a while Dr. Hutchison seemed to do his best, but finally he evidently gave up in despair and sank back in his arm-chair, went sound asleep, and slept peacefully, if not quietly, through the remainder of the examination. It is strange what we remember as we go through life.

Rev. William Thomas Hall, D.D., of the class of 1854, was one of the Trustees in 1903. He was a distinguished minister, who after-wards became professor of Theology in Columbia Theological Semi-nary, and Moderator of our General Assembly. He was one of the most solemn-looking men I ever saw, and yet behind all his solem-nity there was a quiet sense of humor.

Rev. R. Z. Johnston, D.D., of the class of 1858, was also a trus-tee. He was the father of our genial friend and trustee, Mr. Joseph B. Johnston, superintendent of the Barium Springs Presbyterian Orphanage. The father, although he was getting along in years, was as friendly and genial as his son.

When I became a trustee in 1903 Mr. R. A. Dunn, of Charlotte, was regarded as one of the younger trustees, being only about forty years of age. He was first elected in 1893 and served as a trustee continuously until his death on February 21, 1945. In 1895 he be-came a member of the Executive Committee of the Trustees and continued a member until he requested to be relieved in 1941. From 1912 to 1940 he was a member of the Finance Committee, and from 1921 to 1940 was chairman of that important committee. From 1929 until 1940 he was president of the Trustees and thereafter president emeritus until his death. No trustee ever served with greater devotion or rendered a larger service to Davidson College.

Upon his death an editorial in the Charlotte *Observer* paid him a well-deserved tribute. Here is a paragraph from the editorial, which filled a column: "Mr. Robert A. Dunn belonged to the nobility—

the nobility of the great who are great because of their goodness. For much of his long life he has moved in this community with a majestic dignity of carriage. People more than merely admired him. They respected him to the point of veneration. It was his goodness which inspired them, the cleanness of his life, the soft refinement of his nature, and the high range of his ideals . . . He carried his Christian ideals wheresoever he went, whether to the bank of which he was president so many years, whether to the business house that bears his name as the oldest firm in Charlotte, or whether to his home or within the circle of his friends and acquaintances, or certainly to his church toward which he manifested a profound fidelity."

Other members of the Trustees of that time were: Hon. T. B. Fraser, justice of the Supreme Court of South Carolina; Hon. W. F. Stevenson, member of the United States Congress; Hon. Augustus Leazer, member of the North Carolina legislature, and speaker of the house; Hon. B. R. Lacy, treasurer of the State of North Carolina; Dr. William E. Boggs, chancellor of the University of Georgia; and Mr. George W. Watts, capitalist and philanthropist of Durham, North Carolina. At that time there was a total of fifty-six trustees. I have mentioned only a few. There were other names equally venerable and equally impressive.

That was the Board of which I became a member in 1903. I had the feeling expressed by Mr. H. Smith Richardson about twenty years later. He became a trustee in 1922. In his maiden speech he urged that the students of Davidson College be allowed to have their dances on the campus. When he was through, Rev. Dr. D. I. Craig, the venerable pastor of the Presbyterian Church in Reidsville, North Carolina, "took him for a ride." He expressed amazement that the grandson and namesake of Dr. J. Henry Smith, the great preacher and pastor of the First Presbyterian Church of Greensboro, North Carolina, for many years, should advocate such a measure. In his speech Dr. Craig did a very thoroughgoing job. There was not a hoof left behind. As Mr. Richardson and I walked away after adjournment, with a quizzical smile he said: "I wonder how I ever got on this Board. The rougher element must have risen up and demanded representation." That is about the way I felt as I became a member of the august body.

It is not my purpose in these memories to recount all the actions of the Trustees, year after year, for the forty-odd years that have elapsed since 1903, but perhaps you will be interested in a few of the things that especially interested me, as a new member, during the first two or three meetings that I attended.

The most interesting thing that came before the Trustees in 1903 was what, for lack of a better name, we may call "The Freshman Rebellion." The largest class in the history of the college up to that time entered Davidson in the fall of 1902. As we look back over the years we can see now that there were quite a number of notable men in that class. Here are just a few of them: E. J. Erwin, now a professor in Davidson College; Frank L. Jackson, the efficient treasurer of Davidson College since 1913; Benjamin R. Lacy, Jr., president of Union Theological Seminary; J. Oscar Mann, Director of Religious Education in the Synod of North Carolina; Hamilton W. McKay, distinguished physician and trustee of Davidson College; John Walker Moore, Dean of Medical College, Louisville, Kentucky; William M. Fetzer, noted athletic coach; H. Smith Richardson, successful business man and trustee of Davidson College; Bernard R. Smith, distinguished physician of Asheville; and Henry T. Mills, successful business man of Greenville, South Carolina. There are also other well-known names in that class.

As the class was so much larger than usual, the upper classes, especially the sophomores, thought they ought to work very diligently to keep the freshmen in their place. So from the discussions I gathered that there was more hazing than usual and some of it was unnecessarily severe. To make matters worse the freshman baseball team beat the sophomore team. Worse still, the freshman numerals were chalked on the large pillars of the Old Chambers Building. The friction between the freshmen and the upper classes, especially the sophomores, became acute. At length about the middle of February, 1903, the freshmen, feeling that they were not getting a fair deal from the upper classes, decided to leave college. In order to attract as little attention as possible they planned to meet at Cornelius, a mile south of Davidson, and take the train there for their respective homes. Practically all the members of the class turned up at Cornelius shortly before the train going towards Charlotte was due. There was great excitement at the college when the faculty and students learned what was happening. Certain members of the faculty went at top speed to Cornelius. Fortunately the train was an hour or so late. After the members of the faculty had exhorted the freshmen and at the same time promised that they should have a fair deal if they would return to the college, the freshmen yielded and slowly made their way back to the campus.

The whole situation was so serious that the Executive Committee of the Trustees was called to meet at the college to help solve the problem. However, it takes several days to secure a constitutional meeting of the Executive Committee. When the members of the committee arrived matters had been amicably adjusted and all was quiet on the western front. The committee made this report about the matter at the 1903 meeting of the Trustees: "During the first part of the year there were some disorders in college, arising from friction between the freshman class and the higher classes in regard to the courtesies usual between the different classes. The Executive Committee met at the college in order to render any assistance that might be necessary but found that the entire matter had been satisfactorily adjusted, and after hearing the reports, decided that no action was required by them, and that the best interests of the college would be subserved by allowing the entire matter to be passed over without further inquiry." Wise committee. But of course the trustees had a lot of questions to ask members of the committee.

It would have been high tragedy if that large and splendid freshman class had left the college. It would certainly have been high tragedy for the college, and would probably have been high tragedy for some members of the class. The fact that the train was an hour late saved the day. Was that just an accident or was it a part of the Presbyterian doctrine of predestination? It is interesting to look at the roll of the sophomore class for that year. Some of them have reached positions of great distinction. One is a member of the United States Congress; another is one of the most distinguished surgeons in the United States Army; another is a distinguished preacher and professor in a Theological Seminary; and still another is among the top men in what is probably the largest industrial and commercial enterprise in North Carolina. There is no telling what a sophomore may come to.

At that 1903 meeting President Smith told the Trustees about the newly organized Davidson League with great enthusiasm. In a moving address before the Synod of North Carolina in the fall of 1902, he incidentally told the Synod that he was planning to organize the Davidson League, to be composed of all the alumni and friends of the college who would promise to give the college at least ten dollars a year. When he had concluded his address a member of the Synod jumped up and moved that they begin the Davidson League then and there. Before Synod adjourned forty-two members had enrolled. At the meeting of the Trustees at the next commencement, President Smith reported that he had received $1,315 in cash up to that time. That indicated a membership of at least 130. Within two years the membership had reached 400. That seems to have been the maximum. When the intensive campaign for large sums began a few years later, the membership of the League naturally began to fall off. But this special contribution, of approximately four thousand dollars a year for several years, enabled President Smith to make many needed improvements around the college. The Davidson League was the forerunner of the Living Endowment plan which was inaugurated about thirty-two years later, and which is still rendering a large service to the college.

It was the 1903 meeting of the Trustees that authorized President Smith to put in a complete electric system for the college grounds and buildings as soon as he could raise the money for it. This was authorized without opposition and the system was installed before the next annual meeting of the Trustees.

At the 1903 meeting President Smith was authorized to construct an athletic field on "a tract of land lying across the railroad," or at some other suitable location. Within a year the money had been contributed by Mr. W. H. Sprunt of Wilmington, North Carolina, and the Sprunt Athletic Field was under construction on the site now occupied by the Richardson Athletic Stadium.

There were other improvements recommended by President Smith at the 1903 meeting. The new president's mind was full of ideas and plans. In the meantime he was bubbling over with an enthusiasm that was contagious. Davidson College was entering upon a new era. At the close of that meeting, to my utter amazement, I was put on the Executive Committee of the Trustees. That meant that I was expected to take an active part in the work of the Board.

Now let us skip to the next annual meeting of the Trustees at the 1904 commencement. I was appointed to prepare the annual letter which the Trustees were accustomed to send to all the controlling presbyteries in those days. I prepared the letter with some care, and told the exact condition of the college as I saw it. In response to the enthusiastic campaign for new students by the new president, Davidson had enrolled more students than ever before in the history of the college. But unfortunately we did not have adequate dormitory space for them, and we were taking funds from the Endowment and erecting dormitories as an investment, a thing that we would not have been compelled to do if the Church had given adequate support to the college. Not only so, but the annual budget was meeting expenses in a very meagre way and sometimes there were deficits. In the meantime there was need for an enlarged faculty to teach the increasing number of students, but there was no money to employ new professors.

When I read the letter to the Trustees some of the more conservative members grew excited. We should never tell the Church such things even if they were true. Such things should be kept "sub silentio." Some of the trustees, especially those belonging to the legal profession, loved to use Latin phrases in those days. Very few of the brethren knew what they meant, but they sounded scholarly. A motion was promptly made to refer the letter back to me for revision in the light of what had been said. I asked to be excused, as I thought we should tell the Church the plain facts about the college as we saw them. I was not prepared to write a letter that dealt in glittering generalities. So the letter was referred to Dr. Rumple to make such revisions as he thought wise.

I have referred to this incident because it illustrates the change that has taken place. For years now, the Trustees and Administration have been telling the Church not only the truth but the whole truth about the college. The Latin phrase "sub silentio" and all its implications have disappeared.

The liveliest discussion at the 1904 meeting was concerning a request made by President Smith. He had completed the new electric plant which had been authorized by the Trustees for the purpose of lighting the campus and college buildings. At the 1904 meeting President Smith requested the Trustees to authorize him to sell current to boarding houses and such other townspeople as might want it. He had already made the request of the Executive Committee, but the Executive Committee declined to grant it. Instead the Committee took this action as recorded in the minutes: "This recommendation of the President is referred to the Board for consideration *de novo,* inasmuch as the act is *ultra vires.*" I still remember how those delicious Latin phrases were used in the spirited discussions that took place in the meeting of the Trustees. There were two arguments against granting the president's request. One was that our electric current might kill somebody downtown and a suit for indemnity might bankrupt the college. But the main argument adduced was that it was entirely *ultra vires.* The legislature of North Carolina had granted the college a charter to educate young men and not to generate and sell electricity. Such a thing was *ultra vires,* beyond the authority granted by the legislature, and the first thing we knew the legislature would be revoking our charter. While the discussion was pending we took recess for lunch.

Governor Charles B. Aycock of North Carolina was making the commencement oration at Davidson that year and at the same time receiving an LL.D. from the college. Some of us went to him during recess, told him of the discussion, especially the part that centered about the *ultra vires* feature of the charter, and asked if there were any danger of the legislature revoking our charter. I can see him yet as he threw his head back and laughed. Then he said that if the legislature were going to do a thing like that they would have to begin with their own University at Chapel Hill, for the University was already doing the thing we were proposing to do. When we reported this to the Trustees after lunch President Smith's request was granted without further discussion. Even the Latin phrases could not stop him. Nobody was killed and the legislature did not revoke our charter. I have heard of an elderly lady who said that those people who say that worrying does no good are mistaken. She had never worried about anything real hard in her life that it ever happened.

Governor Aycock made a great address at the 1904 commencement. He is known to this day as the educational governor of North Carolina. His address was a plea for universal education. I still remember one of his illustrations. He said that the well-to-do were often interested in the education of their own children, but not in the education of the poor. He reminded the well-to-do that if they wanted their children to attain their best they would have to raise the whole level of education by educating all. An artist will never reach his best until a generation has arisen that is sufficiently educated to appreciate his art. A musician will never reach his best until there is a generation that can appreciate his music. For example, he said that a musically gifted girl will take her seat at the piano and play by the hour while her lover stands by her side and tells her she plays like a seraph. However, that same girl closes the piano several months after her marriage and seldom opens it. Some people think that her household duties have crowded out her music. But that is not it. Her lover no longer stands by the piano to tell her how wonderfully she plays. Instead he is absorbed in his newspaper. Worse still, she discovers that he does not know the difference between "Yankee Doodle" and "Old Hundred."

At the 1904 meeting of the Trustees an important step was taken which caused a warm discussion and some heartburnings. For many years the financial affairs of the college had been managed in the following manner. There was a Treasurer and a Finance Committee who looked after investing the Endowment. Then it was the duty of the Treasurer to collect the income from the Endowment and pay it out as long as he had any income left. At the college one of the professors served as Bursar. It was his duty to collect all student fees, and such other income as might accrue in or around the college. And then it was his duty to pay out the income from these sources as long as he had any left. They made separate reports to the Trustees and these reports were not always combined, and it would have taken a Philadelphia lawyer to tell whether the current expense account had a balance or was running a deficit. From 1879 to 1904 the Treasurer lived in Salisbury, the Finance Committee was located in Charlotte, and the Bursar was at Davidson. All honor to all three of these groups. They rendered valiant service. Especial honor is due to the memory of Mr. S. H. Wiley of Salisbury, who served as Treasurer from 1879 to 1894; of Mr. O. D. Davis of Salisbury, who served as Treasurer from 1894 to 1904; and of Col. W. J. Martin of Davidson, who served as Bursar from 1870 to 1895.

By 1904 the affairs of the college had multiplied to such an extent that it did not seem to be possible any longer to conduct the finances by this three-cornered method. So motion was made to combine the two offices of Treasurer and Bursar, and to elect Dr. John L. Douglas, professor of Mathematics in the college, as head of the office thus created. Dr. Douglas was an unusually good business man and knew his mathematics. That motion provoked a long and heated discussion. Every group I have ever worked with has contained some members who were constitutionally opposed to disturbing the *status quo*, and it is often well. They keep wild-eyed revolutionists from running away with themselves and everybody else. But finally the motion was carried, and Dr. John L. Douglas served the college in a highly efficient way as Treasurer and Bursar from 1904 to 1913.

By 1913 the work of Treasurer and Bursar had grown to such an extent that it was impossible for a professor to carry it any longer as a side line. Dr. Douglas asked to be relieved. Mr. Frank L. Jackson was elected as Treasurer and Business Manager, a position which he continues to fill with distinction to this good hour. Very few if any have rendered a larger service to Davidson College than Mr. Jackson.

Having thus given my first impressions of the Trustees, and some of my observations and experiences in the first two meetings that I attended, it may now be proper for me to make some general observations concerning trustees, after having served as one for twenty-six years, and after having co-operated with the Trustees as the president of the college for nearly twelve years.

It is amazing that any man should think that he is qualified to be a trustee of a great institution without any previous preparation. It takes a man many years to prepare for a professorship in such an institution, and yet it is expected that trustees without any previous preparation should step in and take oversight of a great institution and of a faculty composed of highly trained men. I know now that when I was elected a trustee I had no preparation or qualifications for such a responsible position. Every trustee should use every means available to prepare himself for the duties of his office. There are good books and pamphlets setting forth the qualifications and duties of trustees. The late Dr. Frazer Hood of the Davidson faculty prepared such a pamphlet for the Presbyterian Educational Association of the South in 1941. Trustees would find it helpful to study this pamphlet.

Presbyteries, synods, and other electing bodies are not always as careful in selecting trustees as they should be. Too often they select a man to honor him or to bestow some favor upon him, without seriously inquiring into his qualifications for such a position. Those bodies which have the responsibility of electing trustees for an institution like Davidson College should select the best possible men. It might be well for electing bodies to set an age limit for the retirement of trustees, just as we now have an age limit for the retirement of pastors and professors. I recall being at the commencement of a great institution north of the Mason and Dixon Line when the Board met. It seemed to me that I had never seen such a group of aged and decrepit-looking men brought together before. One or two were in rolling chairs.

Trustees should not legislate about the details involved in the running of an institution. For example, the Davidson Trustees voted to allow seniors to wear caps and gowns. On another occasion the

Trustees voted that the Christmas holidays recess might be length-ened a day or two so that students who wished might attend the Atlanta Exposition. When the Davidson Presbyterian Church got a new organ the Trustees solemnly voted that the college might sell the church a sufficient amount of water to run the motor at ten cents per thousand gallons. In 1921 and again in 1922 the Trus-tees adopted the most elaborate rules for the governing of the fra-ternities. These rules dealt with eligibility for membership, the time of initiation, the time of opening and closing the fraternity houses, chaperons, and many other details. It seems to me that such de-tails of internal administration should be decided by the president and the faculty of the college.

What, then, are the functions of the Trustees? They should first of all elect the president of the college. That is one of the greatest responsibilities that the Trustees have, for the president has much to do in determining the ideals, standards, objectives, and morale of the college. Under the leadership of the president the Trustees should elect the professors and administrative officers of the college. That is also a great responsibility. Practically everything depends upon the kind of president and faculty an institution has.

The Trustees should determine the general policies and objectives of the college, and then charge the administration and faculty with the responsibility of working out the details involved in the policies and objectives. The Trustees are especially responsible for the finan-cial well-being of their institution all along the line. They can also help turn the attention of the choicest high school boys in their churches and communities toward the college. They can interest the people of their churches and communities in Christian educa-tion in general and in their own college in particular.

The ideal for any institution is that the trustees, administration, faculty, students, alumni, and patrons should all work together in perfect harmony for the well-being of their institution and for the accomplishment of its objectives. To my mind the chief objective of a Christian college is to train Christian leaders for the church, the state, and for all walks of life. Davidson has not yet reached abso-lute perfection along these lines, but it is moving in that direction.

VIII ❧ A New Era

IT CAN BE SEEN from the foregoing chapters that with the beginning of a new century and a new administration a new era dawned for the college. It took the South a long time to recover from the destruction and poverty caused by the War Between the States. From the close of the war to 1900 the college remained almost static so far as endowment, buildings, the number of professors, and the number of students were concerned. A few figures will illustrate this.

Only one new building was erected on the campus between 1860 and 1900. That was Morrison Hall, which was used as a gymnasium and Y.M.C.A. building. It was torn down in 1945. The total cost of this building was about four thousand dollars. In 1867 the endowment was reported as approximately $181,000. Of this, $139,000 was invested in eight per cent railroad bonds. In 1869 these railroad bonds were sold for $70,000, and the total endowment was reported as $97,000. In 1900 the endowment was $115,000.

For the session of 1869-70 there were seven members of the faculty and 125 students. In 1900 there were seven members of the faculty plus one instructor, and 131 students not counting the students of the old Medical College, who took one or two courses in Davidson College.

As stated in a previous chapter, Dr. J. B. Shearer resigned in 1900 and Dr. Henry Louis Smith was elected president. However, he did not enter upon the duties of the office until 1901, as he requested that he might have a year to prepare himself for the presidency. He had served as vice-president since 1896, and in that office had performed many of the duties belonging to the president's office, owing to the advancing age and infirmities of the president.

Dr. Smith was the first layman to fill the president's office. Prior to 1901 all the presidents were Presbyterian ministers. He was only forty-one years of age at the time of his election. Dr. Robert Hall Morrison, the first president, was the only one of all the presidents elected at an earlier age than that. He was only thirty-eight. The new president was a scholarly, energetic, enthusiastic man, and full of plans and ideas.

As stated above, the college entered upon a new era with the coming of the new century and a new administration. First of all there was a vigorous campaign for students. As a result the student body grew rapidly. The catalogue for 1905-1906 lists 257 students, exclusive of students from the old Medical College, and of these 243 were studying for regular college degrees.

The increased student body called for new buildings and equipment and for a larger faculty. Between 1900 and 1906 the following buildings were erected: Martin Chemical Laboratory (1901); Shearer Hall (which was a reconstruction of the old chapel in 1901); Rumple Dormitory (1903); and Watts Dormitory (1906). In addition to these buildings an electric light plant and power house was constructed and the Sprunt Athletic Field completed. There were many other minor improvements. Considerable sums of money were raised to finance all these buildings, but not enough. The Trustees accordingly directed that money be taken from the Endowment Fund for the erection of Rumple Dormitory as that could be regarded as an investment. Accordingly we find that in 1906 the Endowment amounted to only $90,000. Incidentally I may mention that in 1906 I was elected president of the Trustees, and continued to fill that position until I was elected president of the college in 1929.

The next big movement in the new era was a financial campaign to increase the Endowment and provide further improvements in buildings and equipment. In 1902 the General Education Board was organized in New York, by Mr. John D. Rockefeller, Sr. This Board was incorporated by an act of Congress on January 12, 1903. From first to last Mr. Rockefeller turned over to that Board approximately $180,000,000. Dr. Wallace Buttrick, a well-known Baptist minister, was appointed secretary and executive officer of the Board. Mr. Rockefeller himself was a member of the Baptist Church. Dr. Buttrick was an affable, genial man, noted for his common sense. He also had a keen sense of humor.

It was the wish of Mr. Rockefeller that Dr. Buttrick should first of all make a general survey of the educational situation throughout the country, with especial emphasis upon the South, which had suffered so severely from the War Between the States. While he was doing this, the endowment which Mr. Rockefeller placed with the General Education Board would be producing an income.

Very soon after the General Education Board was ready for business President Smith applied for an appropriation with the understanding that the friends of Davidson would match it with a similar amount or more. Dr. Buttrick came to Davidson to make a study of the college in person. Being a minister he understood church-related colleges and their ideals, and was in full sympathy with the work they were doing. After studying the situation, Dr. Buttrick suggested that Davidson College should move to Charlotte. In those days there were no good roads, and no automobile or bus service, and the train service was very poor. Davidson was somewhat isolated. It was Dr. Buttrick's opinion that sooner or later every city of the size of Charlotte would have its own college, and Davidson should get in on the ground floor. He pointed out the educational and cultural advantages of Charlotte.

Dr. Buttrick went even further. He suggested the ways and means by which such a move could be accomplished. He thought Charlotte should contribute $200,000 and a site. The General Education Board would give $100,000. Then the college should raise $200,000, one-half of which he thought could be raised in New York.

The suggested removal to Charlotte caused a good deal of excitement and no little discussion. There were many pros and cons, and some warm protests. I remember especially a very warm letter which was addressed to me as president of the Trustees by Dr. Charles G. Vardell of the class of 1888, the president of Flora Macdonald College. He stated that his coat was off, his sleeves up, and he was ready to fight the proposal. I wrote him suggesting that he keep his shirt on and put his coat back on, as there was very little probability that the college would move to Charlotte.

As a matter of fact, Charlotte blocked the movement when the business men seemed to think that $50,000 would be the maximum they could raise. The idea of giving $200,000 and a site was unthinkable. But even if Charlotte had offered to raise the whole amount and more, it is not likely that the Trustees and presbyteries would have consented to the removal. When an institution has been located at a place for threescore and ten years, its roots have gone very deep. I saw that illustrated when the question of removing Union Theological Seminary from Hampden-Sydney to Richmond, Virginia, was under discussion between 1895 and 1898. I was connected with the Seminary at that time, first as a student and then as an instructor. I had never dreamed before how deeply the emotions of good and perfectly sane people could be stirred by the suggestion that an old institution should be moved to a new location.

Dr. Buttrick's suggestion of the removal to Charlotte was not the first time such a suggestion had been made. In the *Davidson Monthly* of May, 1888, there is an editorial on the subject. By the way, Dr. Vardell was one of the student editors at that time. The editorial begins thus: "Not long since we saw in the Charlotte *Chronicle* that the people of Charlotte would offer the college fifty thousand dollars to have Davidson removed to Charlotte. How true this is we cannot say; but since this publication we have often heard this offer discussed by the students, and they are, as a rule, very much in favor of the removal." The author of the editorial was evidently in favor of the proposition and gave a number of reasons. Among other things he said: "In the ante bellum days when the culture, education, and refinement of the South belonged to the large planters, and when these planters lived much after the manner of the ancient feudal lords, then it was proper to have colleges in the country, but now all this has changed. Education, culture, and refinement have almost left the country and gone to the city." There were too many country boys at Davidson to let that pass. So in the issue of the *Davidson Monthly* for June, 1888, there is a warm reply to that editorial, and reasons cited why the college should remain at Davidson.

I do not remember to have had any strong convictions one way or the other when the proposal was made to move to Charlotte. There was something to be said on both sides. But as I look back over the years and at the present situation I have a strong conviction that it was far better for the college to have remained here. Davidson is no longer isolated. There is a network of good automobile roads leading in all directions. There are frequent bus schedules that lead in all directions, including through buses running from New York to Florida and to Atlanta and the Southwest. Davidson has water and light systems that are as good as those of any city. There is an up-to-date dial telephone system by which we can get in touch with any part of the United States in a very few minutes. In addition to all these, we have our radios which keep us in touch with every part of the world. In short, it seems to me that Davidson College is ideally located at present for the carrying out of its ideals and objectives. The present buildings and equipment are probably far better than anything that Dr. Smith and Dr. Buttrick even dreamed of when they were planning for a greater and better Davidson.

When the suggested removal to Charlotte did not work Dr. Buttrick came back with another proposal. He suggested that the college start out to raise $300,000, of which the General Education Board would give $75,000. As the college had already begun a campaign for funds and had raised $70,000, Dr. Buttrick was generous enough to let that be a part of the amount the college was to raise. That meant that it would be necessary for the college to raise only $155,000 additional in order to secure the $75,000 from the General Education Board.

The General Education Board attached several very reasonable conditions to the offer. Of the $300,000 raised, $225,000 had "to be invested and preserved inviolably for endowment." It could not be used for the erection of dormitories or any other improvement. The remaining $75,000 could be used for buildings and equipment. "No part of the income from the sum contributed by the General Education Board should ever be used for specifically theological instruction." There was also a time limit set to the campaign. The document making this appropriation and setting forth the conditions was officially issued by the General Education Board in New York, March 31, 1909. The negotiations leading up to this appropriation had covered a period of several years. In the meantime, as intimated above, the college had been going on with its own campaign.

The Hugh A. and Jane Parks Grey Memorial Library

Between Classes . . . a Welcome Pause

You might suppose that the Trustees of the college would have jumped at the proposition made by the General Education Board, but they did not. Mature Presbyterians are not easily stampeded, and are accustomed to look before leaping. There was plenty of discussion. Some of the brethren felt that this might be a kind of Trojan horse, or perhaps the camel's nose. After full discussion the vote was taken. The minutes say that Dr. William T. Hall asked to be excused from voting and that Hon. T. B. Fraser, justice of the Supreme Court of South Carolina, voted "No." All the other trustees voted in the affirmative.

In May, 1908, President Smith requested the Trustees to appoint a committee to co-operate with him in securing a Field Agent to assist him in prosecuting the financial campaign. Dr. Thomas W. Lingle of the class of 1893 was secured with the understanding that in due time he would be elected to a full professorship in the college. After his graduation, Dr. Lingle took a postgraduate year at Davidson. After that he majored in History and Philosophy at Cornell University. From Cornell he went to Germany where he received the degree of Ph.D. from Leipsic University in 1898. Returning to the United States he studied at Union Theological Seminary in Virginia and at Princeton, graduating from Princeton Seminary in 1901. Then he took a contract to teach History and Philosophy in Mackenzie College, Sao Paulo, Brazil, for three years. After that he was president of Blackburn College in Illinois for four years. From Blackburn College he came to Davidson in 1908. It can be seen that he had a rather unusual educational background. He had a very retentive memory, and as he continued to read and travel widely through the years, he became one of the best informed men I have ever known.

As Field Agent, Dr. Lingle did some heroic work for two and a half or three years. It is never an easy task to raise money, and it was far more difficult in those days than it is now. Besides, the country passed through a severe financial panic in 1907 and 1908. I was living in Atlanta at that time and recall how the banks would let us draw out only a few dollars at a time, and how the Atlanta Clearing House issued token money to be used locally. In 1910 Dr.

Lingle was elected professor of Modern Languages, but continued to serve a year or two longer as Field Agent. Later he was transferred to the chair of European History and continued to serve the college with distinction until his sudden death on March 26, 1937.

Notwithstanding the fact that he had secured a Field Agent, President Smith continued to prosecute the financial campaign vigorously in person. Among other things he went to see Mr. Andrew Carnegie, who was at that time donating funds for libraries in cities and colleges. In response Mr. Carnegie gave Davidson College twenty thousand dollars for the erection of a library. This building was erected just east of where the old Steward's Hall stood, and was completed in 1910. As a result, Steward's Hall, one of the landmarks, was removed. Another dormitory was needed. Dr. Smith went into Georgia, which was then a part of the constituency of Davidson, and solicited funds. He received a sufficient amount to justify naming the new building the Georgia Dormitory. It was built of light brick and completed in 1909. Why it was built of light brick when all the other buildings were of red brick has always remained a mystery to me, just as it has been a mystery why they used light stucco on Shearer Hall. There is no accounting for tastes.

In due time, the financial campaign was completed, and besides the new buildings mentioned above and other improvements, the endowment of the college had reached approximately the sum of $275,000. That was a big advance over anything the college had ever known before, and Dr. Buttrick and the General Education Board had made it possible by their contribution and their encouragement. From that day to this the General Education Board has been a friend to Davidson College, and has contributed a sum total of more than $450,000 to the college.

But while this campaign for better equipment and a larger endowment was going forward, the budget for current expenses was not faring so well. At the meeting of the Trustees in 1911 the Treasurer reported a deficit of more than $11,000. In his report to the meeting in 1912 the deficit was still more than $11,000. In the meantime the work of the Treasurer's office had become too heavy for a professor to carry as a side line.

In view of this situation the first thing the Trustees did at the 1912 meeting was to pass this resolution: "That a competent committee of business men be appointed to investigate our present financial methods, compare with those in use in other institutions, confer with the Treasurer, Superintendent and President of the college, and report at the next annual meeting of the Board their conclusions and recommendations." The following committee was appointed: W. J. Roddey, W. H. Sprunt, R. A. Dunn, and G. W. Watts. That was certainly a competent committee. I never knew four finer Christian business men. The work of that committee resulted in the setting up of the office of Treasurer and Business Manager in 1913 with Mr. F. L. Jackson as its head. Under his leadership the Davidson office has become known for its system and efficiency throughout the American college world. Mr. W. J. Roddey of Rock Hill, South Carolina, who was a trustee of the college from 1906 to 1938, deserves the main credit for the creation of this office and its guidance for several years. The Trustees gave him a rising vote of appreciation in 1914, and again in 1915.

During this era there came to President Smith a remarkable offer from a business firm that coveted him for a public relations officer and vice-president. The salary was five times the amount that he was receiving at Davidson, plus a comfortable block of stock. At the head of the firm were three or four extraordinarily fine men, all elders in the Presbyterian Church. The offer gave him a good deal of concern. He had a wife and several small children, and no savings. The matter was never publicized, but he took it up with me as president of the Trustees. I recall that he and I talked it over one night until nearly two o'clock. The one thing that concerned him was his family. What would become of them in case of his death? With the larger salary and a share in the business he could soon make ample provision for them. However, as he thought and prayed over the matter, it did not take him many days to decline the offer. I am sure that he has never regretted his decision. I mention this incident because it has been such loyal devotion on the part of the members of the faculty that is largely responsible for making Davidson College what it is today.

There comes to me a very distinct recollection of an attempt to revise the constitution and by-laws of the Trustees during this period. The college was growing and developing in a way that the original makers had never dreamed. So there was a feeling that the constitution and by-laws should be readjusted to meet the needs of the growing college. They made me chairman of the committee. We did some hard work. Before the next meeting of the Trustees we printed the proposed revision, leaving every other page blank, and sent a copy to each trustee with the request that they write suggestions on the blank pages and send them to us for further revision. We got very few suggestions, but when the Trustees met in 1911 there was quite a stir. I do not recall that our committee did anything radical, but some trustees thought so. Some of the trustees sent out and got Dr. Shearer, the venerable ex-president, and several of the more conservative members of the faculty. They were given the privileges of the floor, and they did a plenty to our proposed revision. There was a lot of warm discussion before lunch and after. This quotation from the minutes shows the conclusion of the whole matter: "After a protracted discussion, it was moved and seconded that the Board re-affirm the old constitution and discharge the committee, with its thanks to the committee for its diligent and faithful work on the proposed revision." And that was that. I wish that I had a copy of that proposed revision so that I could see how progressive or revolutionary it looks in the year 1946.

Later on in that same meeting it was voted that "a committee be appointed to recommend *needed* amendments to the constitution and by-laws." That carried the soft impeachment that some of the recommendations made by the committee of which I had been chairman were not needed. As presiding officer it fell to my lot to appoint the new committee. I appointed Drs. W. J. McKay and C. M. Richards and Mr. James W. Pharr. There was nothing radical in the recommendations they made at the next meeting.

In 1912, Dr. Henry Louis Smith, who had been president of Davidson for eleven years, was elected president of Washington and Lee University, and after mature deliberation accepted. His letter of resignation is a very interesting document, covering nearly two typewritten pages in the minutes of the Trustees. In response the Trustees passed resolutions covering nearly a page, in which they paid a handsome tribute to the retiring president. Here are one or two excerpts: "His administration has been attended with great success. By his indomitable energy, as well as by his strong personality, he has developed the efficiency of the college, until it now occupies a commanding place among the educational institutions of our country.

"The material developments are apparent to the most casual observers, and are somewhat of a wonder to students who have attended the college in former years . . . In numbers the student body has grown from about 100, or less, to 343. Our dormitories are crowded and many students have been declined. The curriculum has been broadened and the educational standard of the college has been considerably raised."

The Trustees went at once into the election of a new president. The Executive Committee had paved the way. At that time the constitution required that public notice be given, through the papers, two months prior to the election of a president or professor. As Dr. Smith had notified the Executive Committee several months in advance, the committee gave the public notice so that all who wished might make nominations. By the time the Trustees met, the Executive Committee had quite a goodly list of names. I recall that there were an unusual number of letters advocating the election of a well-known and able Presbyterian minister. Some friend must have been at work, it may have been without the knowledge of the minister. But the friend evidently did not know Presbyterian psychology. A concerted effort like that usually sends Presbyterians in the opposite direction. Before the vote was taken a resolution was passed requiring at least a two-thirds majority to elect any man. On the first ballot Dr. W. J. Martin, who had filled the chair of Chemistry for seventeen years, received more than the necessary two-thirds and was elected. He entered upon the duties of the president's office on June 1, 1912.

Dr. Martin was a man of forceful personality, intellectual vigor, and deep religious convictions. He had many of the traits of his noble father, Colonel W. J. Martin, but lacked the merry twinkle which his father had in his left eye. He promptly took up the work where Dr. Smith had left off, and carried it forward with great energy and resolution. The first thing to be done was to find a professor of Chemistry to fill the place made vacant by Dr. Martin's election to the presidency. Temporary arrangements were made, but in February, 1913, a special meeting of the Trustees was called at which time Dr. H. B. Arbuckle, professor of Chemistry in Agnes Scott College, was unanimously elected.

Dr. Arbuckle was born near Lewisburg, West Virginia, graduated from Hampden-Sydney College in 1890, and after that took his Ph.D. degree in Chemistry at Johns Hopkins. He taught for a while in the State College for Women, Tallahassee, Florida. From there he went to Agnes Scott College in 1898. Coming to Davidson in 1913 he was the senior professor of Chemistry from that time until his retirement in 1937, when he was made professor emeritus. In addition to filling his chair with great acceptability, Dr. Arbuckle took a large interest in the spiritual welfare of the students.

Somehow I think of Dr. Arbuckle as the last one of the "old guard," consisting of a dozen outstanding professors, each of whom served the college for many years within my memory, and all of whom have been retired, or have passed to their reward. Their names have been mentioned either in previous chapters or in this one. If I do not mention the names of professors who have been elected since 1913, and who are still on active duty, it will not be because of any lack of appreciation, but because it is a little too much like vivisection to talk about men who are still active professors. I think that Davidson still has a great faculty and a great president.

The inauguration of Dr. Martin as president at the commencement of 1913 was a rather modest affair compared with more recent inaugurations. I wonder who invented this modern method of inviting all the colleges in the world to send their presidents to the inauguration of a new president, and if the president could not come to send a dean, and if the dean could not come, to send a professor, and if a professor could not come to send an alumnus who lives near enough to attend. Then when they get them all gowned up for the academic procession you can't tell a president from an alumnus.

All of which reminds me of a story that Dr. C. R. Harding brought back from a meeting of some of the leading classical scholars of America. The president of a civic club telegraphed a college president to send him a speaker. He did not want anyone lower than a dean and would like to have a wit. The college president telegraphed back that the college did not have anybody lower than a dean, and they did not have a wit, but that he could send him two half wits.

At Dr. Martin's inauguration I presided as president of the Trustees, propounded the usual questions, and gave the charge. Dr. J. B. Shearer, the aged vice-president, also gave a charge. He was then over eighty and spoke sitting down. I remember that he apologized by saying that he was weak in his feet and legs, but that he would a great deal rather give way at that end first than at the other end. Then four alumni, from the four classes that were in college with Dr. Martin in his student days, brought brief greetings. Dr. Neal L. Anderson represented the class of 1885; Mr. O. L. Clark the class of 1886; Mr. H. N. Pharr the class of 1887; and Dr. S. R. McKee the class of 1888, which was Dr. Martin's class. Mr. W. S. Golden, of the senior class that year, spoke for the student body. In addition to these brief addresses Dr. Martin made his inaugural address. As I look back over the years at that program it strikes me as a very sensible one. With this auspicious send-off Dr. Martin launched out upon a successful administration, covering a period of seventeen years, the longest administration in the history of the college.

IX ❧ Lights and Shadows

As I THINK over the period covered by this chapter (1912-1929) it seems to me that the above is the most appropriate title. Some dark shadows fell upon the college during this period. There was the terrifying shadow of the World War. That had scarcely passed when the historic Old Chambers Building was utterly destroyed by fire. It had stood there as the very heart of the college for sixty years and more. We had scarcely caught our breath when the Watts Dormitory was burned to the ground.

But there were also some very bright spots during those years. The new Chambers Building was erected. A larger and better Watts Dormitory was built. The student body and faculty grew very much larger. Davidson was named as a beneficiary of the Duke Endowment. The Teachers Annuity Fund was established. The lights eventually banished the shadows.

Sometime after Dr. Martin's election, I suggested to him that the new president of the college might like to have a new president of the Trustees, and told him that I would not only get out of the way, but would help to elect any man he wanted. I knew that he would deal frankly with me, for he was one of the frankest persons I ever knew. He told me that he would like to see Mr. George W. Watts president of the Trustees, but that if he would not accept I was his next choice. I took the matter up very earnestly with Mr. Watts, but he was not willing to even consider the suggestion, saying that he had arrived at the age where he was laying down work instead of taking up new work. He was already president of the Trustees of Union Theological Seminary, and that may have had something to do with his decision. So I was continued as president of the Trustees. Of course, the Trustees had the privilege of electing a new president at any annual meeting, as officers were elected annually.

From 1912 to 1917, the college moved on in the even tenor of its way. Nothing particularly startling happened. The size of the student body and of the faculty remained about the same as it was. The average number of students during these five years was 351. Of these an annual average of 305 were studying for degrees. The

rest were listed as eclectics or specials. There were twelve full professors, one assistant professor, and three instructors in 1912. In
1917, there were thirteen full professors and four associate professors. Although America did not enter the World War until 1917,
the war which had been going on in Europe since August, 1914,
evidently affected the college to a certain extent.

In May, 1914, President Martin, who was not a minister but a
ruling elder, was elected Moderator of the General Assembly of the
Presbyterian Church in the United States, in session in Kansas City.
The friends of the college were delighted by the election of the president to the highest office in the Church. The only previous president of Davidson elected to that office was Dr. John L. Kirkpatrick,
who was Moderator of the General Assembly in 1862 at its meeting
in Montgomery, Alabama. Only one layman, if a ruling elder can
be called a layman, had been previously elected Moderator of the
General Assembly. The election of President Martin to this high
office was a fine tribute to him personally, and meant much to the
college.

The most interesting thing that took place at the college during
these five years, from the point of view of the Trustees, was another
campaign for funds. In May, 1914, the Trustees authorized a campaign for at least $100,000 of which $75,000 was to be used for
endowment and the remainder for buildings and equipment. Appli-
cation was made to the General Education Board for an appropriation. On October 22, 1914, the General Education Board made an
appropriation of $25,000 provided the college would raise at least
$75,000. The Trustees of the college accepted this appropriation
unanimously without question. None of the trustees seemed to be
afraid of a Trojan horse this time.

Dr. C. M. Richards, who was then pastor of the Davidson Presbyterian Church, was elected by the Trustees as Field Agent to help
raise funds to meet the offer of the General Education Board. The
congregation granted him leave of absence for several months, and
he did some valiant work in raising funds for the college. Upon Dr.
Richards' return to his pastorate, the Trustees elected Rev. J. C.
Shive as Field Agent to begin his work on September 1, 1915. Mr.

Shive did some excellent work and raised considerable sums. We should not forget the services of Mr. Shive and other Field Agents, who, in their own modest way, rendered a large service to the college in raising funds to increase the endowment and erect buildings. They had a difficult and thankless task.

In May, 1916, it was reported to the Trustees that the campaign had been successfully completed, whereupon they ordered that $75,000 be added to the endowment, and $25,000 devoted to the erection of a new gymnasium. This amount was used to erect the gymnasium that stands between the Chambers Building and the Richardson Athletic Field. It has never been a satisfactory gymnasium. However, in saying that I am reminded of the little girl who, upon hearing her mother complain about the discomforts of the church and the dullness of the service, said: "Well, Mother, what could you expect for a nickel?" We are all looking forward with joy to the erection of the $250,000 gymnasium now that the war is over.

President Woodrow Wilson paid an unexpected visit to Davidson College on May 20, 1916. He came to Charlotte to take part in the celebration of the one hundred and forty-first anniversary of the Mecklenburg Declaration of Independence. When President Martin heard that he was coming to Charlotte he went to Washington and gave him a cordial and urgent invitation to visit Davidson, but the President would not make any promises. After President Wilson arrived in Charlotte, Dr. Martin went to see him again in person and pressed the invitation, but received no encouragement. Dr. Martin returned to Davidson somewhat crestfallen. A few hours later President and Mrs. Wilson arrived at Davidson unannounced. He was weary and requested that he be allowed to roam around the campus without having to make a talk or to meet the people. He was a student at Davidson during the session 1873-74 and wanted to renew the memories of his student days. Among other things he wanted to visit the room he occupied as a student, number 13 on the first floor of the north wing of the Old Chambers Building.

Ray Stannard Baker, the official biographer of President Wilson, tells, in his first volume, an amusing incident which is alleged to have occurred in connection with his visit to his old room. As stated above, he came to Davidson unannounced and he visited his room unannounced. When he knocked on the door the freshman occupant said: "Come in." The President, not hearing him, knocked a little louder and longer. The freshman, a bit exasperated, shouted: "Come on in. Who are you, anyway?" The President replied: "Woodrow Wilson." The freshman answered: "You've got nothing on me. I'm Christopher Columbus. Come right on in." When the door opened and the freshman saw that it was really President Wilson he gave just one look of anguish and plunged out of the open window.

It is a pity to spoil a good story by saying that it is not accurate in all its details. However, there is a foundation for it. President Wilson did visit his old room unannounced, and the occupant, or occupants, did go out of the window when they realized that the President was coming in, and thereby missed an opportunity of meeting and talking with one of the great men of all time.

Ray Stannard Baker adds this interesting paragraph: "Davidson College always had a warm spot in Wilson's heart. His correspondence of later years shows that he never lost an opportunity to express his affection or to comply with the requests of students or faculty for friendly services. At the inauguration in 1913, a delegation of eighty students from Davidson College marched with the parade down Pennsylvania Avenue, carrying the Davidson banner."

It is strange how rumors persist through the years. Woodrow Wilson attended Davidson during the session 1873-74, and then dropped out of college. A year later he went to Princeton. While I was president of Davidson, letters came to me from time to time inquiring whether it was really true that Woodrow Wilson "flunked out" of Davidson or was expelled for stealing coal. The letters came chiefly from high school boys. Perhaps they were trying to get some comfort. There is not the slightest foundation for the rumors. He dropped out of college and remained out a year because of his health. His grades at Davidson as they appear on the faculty records are the best answer to all such rumors. Here they are. For the first term: Logic and Rhetoric 95, Greek 87, Latin 90, Mathematics

74, Composition 96, Declamation 92, Deportment 100. Second term: English 97, Greek 88, Latin 94, Mathematics 88, Composition 95, Declamation 92, Deportment 100.

It may not be amiss to record here something that Dr. Joseph R. Wilson, the father of Woodrow Wilson, a distinguished Presbyterian minister, wrote concerning Davidson College about ten years after his son was a student here. He wrote as follows: "Were Davidson College to do no more in future years in the way of training our candidates for the ministry, as also in the way of furnishing intelligent recruits for the ranks of our eldership, than it has been doing in the years that are gone, it would continue to rank higher amongst us than any other agency for good in the minds of thoughtful men. Surely if Davidson be not worthy of public favor then no college is."

When the United States entered the World War in April, 1917, Davidson immediately felt the effects. The next year the student body dropped to 321 and the following year to 301. Of course, that was not as serious as what has happened to the college in the Second World War. Between April, 1917, and September, 1918, one hundred and fifty-eight Davidson students enlisted in the service of their country. Members of the faculty also went into the service. Dr. J. W. MacConnell entered the Medical Corps and served in France. He entered as a captain and came out a lieutenant-colonel. Dr. Thomas W. Lingle, beyond the age of active service, entered the service of the Y.M.C.A. in France near Verdun, where he served from September, 1917, to the close of the war. President Martin was eager to go to France as a Y.M.C.A. worker and requested a year's leave of absence, but the Trustees felt that he was needed at the college in those crucial days and persuaded him to remain at home. Also other members of the faculty were called to camps in the homeland, but so far as I can recall or discover, no others went across to France.

The records show that 736 Davidson students and alumni were enlisted in that World War. Of these, twenty laid down their lives, and numbers of others were wounded or disabled by gas. I did not know personally all those who were killed, but I knew some of them intimately, and they were among the noblest young men I ever knew.

You will find their names and photographs in the college library.

On October 1, 1917, the student Army Training Corps was established in the college, and all students over eighteen, a total of 223, were enlisted in it. The Army officers connected with the S.A.T.C. practically took charge of the college from that time until the Armistice was signed on November 11, 1918. That arrangement cut deep into the regular work of the college. During that period a terrible epidemic of the Spanish influenza swept through the college like wild fire. There were more than two hundred and fifty cases in the college. All college exercises were suspended for three weeks. The shadow of the war was hanging dark over the college.

During the emergency caused by the war, it was necessary for the college administration to do a good many things which under normal conditions would have required the approval of the Trustees, or at least of the Executive Committee of the Trustees, which has practically all the powers of the Trustees between the meetings of the full Board. All such steps taken by the administration without the authorization of the Trustees were reported to the Executive Committee at a meeting on October 8, 1918, and the Executive Committee took the following action:

"Be it resolved that the contracts and arrangements as entered into by Dr. Martin relating to the installation of a Student Army Training Corps be and the same are hereby ratified and approved, and full force and effect is given this said act as if the same had been duly and specifically authorized in the first instance, and Dr. Martin as president is further authorized to enter into any further contracts with the Government in order to continue said Student Army Training Corps at the college as may be required by the government, and this said act, when done, shall be in all respects binding upon the college." When that action was taken we little dreamed that the World War would come to a sudden end one month and three days later.

When the Executive Committee next met, on January 24, 1919, the S.A.T.C. had been disbanded, as there was no longer any need for it, and the R.O.T.C. had been established, by the authority given in the above resolution. The college administration was perfectly honest in believing that the above resolution gave such authority, but there were some of us who doubted it, as the resolution referred to the S.A.T.C., which was something very different. As strange as it may seem, there is nowhere recorded in the minutes of the Trustees or of the Executive Committee the contract that was entered into by the government and the college in the establishment of the R.O.T.C.

Immediately upon the close of the World War, the student enrollment shot up. In 1918-19 there were only 301 students. For the session of 1919-20 there were 454, the next year there were 498, and the next 512. By 1924-25 the student body had reached 627. There had never been anything like it in the history of the college. It kept the administration and Trustees busy securing professors, and what is even more, securing funds to pay them. The General Education Board came to the rescue, and, beginning in 1920-21, contributed $8,500 a year to current expenses for three years, and on the fourth year contributed $5,000, making a total of $31,250. That meant a great deal to the college during those years when it was going through acute growing pains.

In the meantime, plans were being made for greatly increasing the endowment of the college. In 1919, Davidson joined with the other Presbyterian colleges of North Carolina in what was known as the Million Dollar Campaign. This campaign was authorized by the Synod of North Carolina. Again Davidson applied to the General Education Board for assistance. On December 4, 1919, the General Education Board offered to give $100,000 to Davidson in a campaign for a total of $450,000. Of this amount, $300,000 was to be added to the endowment and as such preserved inviolate. Again the Trustees accepted this offer with alacrity. There was no discussion and no negative votes this time.

As a result of the million dollar campaign, which was conducted under the leadership of Rev. M. E. Melvin, D.D., Davidson was enabled to meet this offer more promptly than we had even hoped. Thus nearly a half million dollars was added to the assets of the college.

We had scarcely caught our breath when, at a meeting of the Trustees on May 25, 1920, this action was taken: "The president was given authority to accept a proposition of the General Education Board, if made by them, to donate $100,000 to be used in increasing professors' salaries, provided the college will raise a like amount." In response to this request the General Education Board agreed to give $75,000 if the college would raise $125,000. The campaign was completed and the $200,000 thus raised was added to the endowment with the understanding that the income from it would be used to raise the salaries of the professors. Salaries were substantially increased.

From the above sketch it can be seen that the college was going forward at a breath-taking speed during the years immediately after the World War. The student body, the faculty, and the assets of the college grew beyond anything that we had dreamed of only a few years before. It is especially worthy of note that by 1922 the endowment had passed the $600,000 mark. The old college had again taken on new life.

While all this was going on an interesting event took place. The General Assembly of the Presbyterian Church in the United States met in Charlotte in May, 1920. At the meeting of the Trustees in the previous March, President Martin and Dr. C. M. Richards were directed to invite the General Assembly to Davidson, to arrange for a special train to be paid for by the college, and to plan a program. The General Assembly accepted the invitation and on Saturday afternoon, May the twenty-second, the special train brought 307 ministers and elders to Davidson, representing every part of the South. By the way, the train cost $422.10, which was a fine investment from an advertising point of view to say the very least.

There was quite a program at the college, addresses of welcome, responses, and so forth. As I happened to be the Moderator of the General Assembly that year it fell to my lot to make the response. That put me in an embarrassing position. There were plenty of people in the audience who knew me as a freshman. In fact, I had been around Davidson so much that I was as common as corn bread for dinner. I began by saying that my situation reminded me of a

Negro of doubtful character who moved to a distant town and became a preacher. He got along finely until one night as he was about to take his text he saw a well-known Negro from his home town come down the aisle and take a front seat. The preacher rose to the occasion by saying that he was going to do something he had never done before, change his text at the last moment. He said that instead of taking the text in Revelation which he had planned to take he was going to turn back to the book of prophecy of Isaiah and take a text which reads thuswise: "If you know me say nothing, I'll see you later." That was the request I was making of my Davidson friends. When the exercises were over a matter-of-fact lady said to me in all seriousness: "I don't believe that text is in Isaiah." I have often wondered what should be done with people like that.

While the college was thus growing as never before and everything looked rosy there suddenly came one of the greatest disasters in the history of the college. Early Monday morning, about one or two o'clock, November 28, 1921, the old Maxwell Chambers Building was utterly destroyed by fire. It had been the principal building on the campus for more than sixty years. It was a massive, handsome old building and had been the very heart of the college during all those years. The fire occurred on the week end after Thanksgiving. There were an unusual number of guests at Davidson, mostly young people. One way of entertaining guests was to take them up to the cupola of the old building, from which there were wonderful views by day and even by night. It has been generally supposed that some student or visitor in going to the cupola carelessly dropped a lighted match or cigarette stump up in that part of the building where there was inflammable material. There it smoldered until after midnight and then burst into flames.

The president, the faculty, and the students of Davidson College never showed up to finer advantage than on that occasion. When it was seen that nothing could save the building the whole college population gathered near the campus well. President Martin made a ringing address, and they all resolved to stand by each other and by the college in that tragic hour. Then with bowed heads they sang "O Davidson." This scene appears all the more remarkable

FAMOUS FRENCH CRYSTAL CHANDELIER
Dating from the reign of Louis Philippe
(LOCATED IN PHI HALL)

when we remember that one hundred and thirty-three students who roomed in Old Chambers had been burned out of house and home. Places were found for them temporarily by doubling up in other dormitories and by renting rooms in the village.

I was then living in Richmond, and I recall the feeling that came over me as I read the press dispatch telling of the fire. I felt that a great tragedy had taken place and that something very real had gone out of my life. But upon second thought I remarked to my family that I felt sure that in the long run it would prove a blessing in disguise. So it has proven.

As chairman, I called the Executive Committee to meet at the college at noon on November the thirtieth, less than thirty-six hours after the fire. In the meeting the college administration and Executive Committee wrestled with the various problems that confronted us. The erection of temporary buildings was authorized. As a result the wooden barracks known as North and South, and the two-story building just north of the dormitories, now used by the R.O.T.C., were speedily erected. The total cost was reported as approximately $9,000. It was hoped that all those wooden buildings would be temporary, but they stood there for twenty-four years, until they were removed in 1945. Then it was ordered that the insurance money collected should be used in erecting a fireproof dormitory. The insurance, which was collected a little later, amounted to $107,256.53. East and West Dormitories were paid for by this fund supplemented by funds from other sources. The question of providing additional dormitory space was urgent, as there were over 500 students and the only dormitories were Rumple, Watts, and Georgia.

When these emergency measures had been taken, we began to discuss the problem of erecting a new Chambers. There was not a dollar in sight, as the insurance collected was to be used for dormitories. It is interesting to remember that some who were present at that meeting wanted to restore Old Chambers just as it was. The stone foundations were still there. Now as a matter of fact Old Chambers had very little to recommend it as a modern educational building. But sentiment is at times more powerful than logic. Those who favored the restoration of the old building were satisfied with this resolution: "That the Finance Committee be empowered to secure expert advice to lay before the Executive Committee as to the rebuilding of the Chambers Building in a way that will be best suited for the educational needs of the college." In suggesting that resolution, as chairman, I felt sure that no experts would advise the restoration of Old Chambers as it was. For the sake of sentiment we advised that the handsome old pillars remain standing until the new building should be erected. So there they stood making an appeal to all who passed by to do something. That was all for that meeting of the Executive Committee, but it was a good deal.

At the very next meeting of the Executive Committee, on January 25, 1922, it was voted to launch a campaign for one million dollars, to build the new Chambers and to do quite a number of other things that needed to be done. The Trustees at their meeting on February 22, 1922, felt that a million was too large an undertaking, and voted to launch a campaign for $600,000. All the committees and machinery for such a campaign were authorized. The General Education Board again came to the rescue and offered to contribute $100,000 to such a campaign. President Martin was not able to attend that meeting. He and his son were both reported as ill and special prayer was made for them.

The campaign got off to a slow start. The president of the college had his hands full supervising the erection of the temporary buildings and the two new dormitories, besides attending to the usual duties of the president's office. Not only so, but there had recently been several whirlwind campaigns for Davidson, to say nothing of other institutions. Everybody was tired and the people at large were weary of campaigns. Mr. Malcolm Lockhart, Sr., was employed as Field Agent and did excellent work in raising moderate sums here and there. But it takes more than moderate sums to raise $600,000. The college was face to face with a herculean task. But the ruins of Old Chambers made a tremendous appeal to all the friends of Davidson.

As if the college did not have trouble enough, the Watts Dormitory, which had been erected in 1906 largely through the gifts of Mr.

George W. Watts, was burned on Sunday, February 25, 1923, while students and faculty were attending church. Money had to be raised for its restoration. Mrs. John Sprunt Hill, the daughter of Mr. Watts, whose death occurred March 7, 1921, contributed $10,000, and Mrs. Watts, now Mrs. Cameron Morrison, contributed the remainder. The new Watts Dormitory thus constructed is a fire-proof building and considerably larger than the original.

In May, 1922, the Trustees appointed a committee to prepare plans for the new Chambers. In February, 1923, the Trustees authorized the treasurer to borrow $125,000 to be used in the erection of the new building, and in October, 1923, the Executive Committee voted to place the new building slightly back of where the old one had stood. In February, 1924, Mr. Henry C. Hibbs, of Nashville, Tennessee, who had been employed as architect, met with the Executive Committee and stated the problems connected with the planning of the new building. At their meeting on February 27, 1924, the Trustees authorized the president of the college and the building committee to proceed with the construction of the south wing of the new Chambers Building. A special meeting of the Executive Committee was called for April 21, 1924, to request the General Education Board to extend the time limit of their offer of $100,000 to the college as the Davidson Campaign had not raised enough money to claim the appropriation. This the General Education Board graciously did.

As the campaign lagged and the new building was not under way the students got restless. The senior class petitioned the Trustees to do something. They did not know of all that was being done as outlined above. Along this same line, the Executive Committee on November 16, 1926, passed this resolution: "It is the sense of the Executive Committee that the most urgent need of the college at this time is the completion of the new Chambers Building, and that this may be accomplished at an early date Dr. W. J. Martin, president of the college, and Mr. F. L. Jackson, treasurer of the college, be instructed to proceed at once to make every effort possible to secure funds from friends of the college for the purpose of completing same, they to use any members of the faculty they deem wise in helping in the work."

By May, 1927, sufficient funds had been raised to justify the Trustees in passing a resolution authorizing the completion of the Chambers Building. At the same meeting the secretary was instructed "to convey to Dr. Martin, Dr. J. M. McConnell, Dr. C. M. Richards and Mr. F. L. Jackson, the Board's appreciation for the fine work done in securing additional funds for the completion of the Chambers Building." By 1928 sufficient funds had been raised to claim the $100,000 conditionally promised by the General Education Board, and it was promptly paid. In 1929, new Chambers was completed. It had been a long hard pull, but it was worth it, for the new Chambers is one of the best appointed educational buildings in this country. Much praise is due to Mr. Henry C. Hibbs, the architect, and to President Martin for the way in which they labored over blueprints until they got that large building planned to as near perfection as mortal men could hope to make it. Although I have quoted largely from the records, I remember those long and anxious years with great distinctness.

While all those efforts for the erection of the new Chambers were being made, there came an announcement, right out of the blue, that Mr. James Buchanan Duke had set up an endowment on December 11, 1924, amounting to $40,000,000, and that Davidson College was to receive five per cent of the annual income from this endowment. He had not consulted anyone connected with the college or informed anyone of his intentions. From a financial point of view this is the biggest event in the history of the college.

Here is the notice the college received as recorded in the minutes of the Trustees: Extract from Indenture dated December 11, 1924, creating the Duke Endowment, signed by J. B. Duke: "Five per cent of said net amount not retained as aforesaid for addition to the corpus of the trust shall be paid to Davidson College (by whatever name it may be known) now located at Davidson, in the state of North Carolina, so long as it shall not be operated for private gain, to be utilized by said institution for any and all the purposes thereof." That was all, but it was enough to make the friends of Davidson College everlastingly grateful to Mr. Duke, and to God who must have put it into his heart to do this thing.

It is interesting to note the various causes and institutions which were named by Mr. Duke as beneficiaries of the income from the endowment. First of all, twenty per cent of the income is to be added to the principal until it reaches eighty million dollars. Of the remainder of the income thirty-two per cent goes to Duke University; five per cent to Davidson College; five per cent to Furman University, Greenville, South Carolina; four per cent to Johnson C. Smith University, a Negro institution, Charlotte, North Carolina; thirty-two per cent to hospitals; ten per cent to orphanages, white and colored; two per cent to superannuated Methodist ministers and to widows and orphans of deceased ministers; six per cent for the erection of Methodist churches in rural districts; and four per cent for the maintenance and support of Methodist churches in rural districts. If you wish to estimate approximately what each of these institutions and causes have received on an average annually since the endowment was established nearly twenty years ago, take $14,000 as representing one per cent. Much larger provision was made for Duke University by other gifts and by the last will and testament of Mr. Duke.

There is one part of the Indenture creating the endowment that should not be overlooked. It reads thus: "As respects any year or years and any purpose or purposes for which this trust is created (except payments hereinafter directed to be made to Duke University) the trustees (of the endowment) in their uncontrolled discretion may withhold the whole or any part of said incomes, revenues and profits which would otherwise be distributed under the fifth division hereof." The fifth division is the division under which the distributions named above are made.

This withholding power was no doubt given to the trustees of the Duke Endowment so that they might have power to deal with the situation if any of these institutions or agencies should go out of existence or prove unworthy. It does give the power to the trustees to cut off any institution or any agency if it should seem best to them.

The Trustees of the college promptly appointed a committee to go to Charlotte where Mr. Duke was living at the time to express the appreciation of the college in person. President Martin was made chairman of the committee, but for some reason he could not go, and I, as president of the Trustees, was appointed to take his place. I went with a good deal of trepidation. I had never seen Mr. Duke and was not accustomed to associate with captains of industry. A little speech of appreciation was prepared with care, but I never got to make it. Mr. Duke received us with such cordiality that we were at once at our ease, and got our appreciation across in a perfectly natural way without making any prepared speeches.

Mr. Duke was a large man, over six feet in height and well built. He had a massive head and a full face. His hair was reddish and his complexion somewhat florid. All told he was a very impressive personality. The part of the conversation that I remember most distinctly was the part in which he told us how he would run a college. He was not a college man himself, though he did attend Guilford for a few months before it was a real college.

Among other things, Mr. Duke said that if he were president of a college and was not sure about the efficiency of a professor he would visit his class for an hour. If he was not satisfied he would make another visit in a month or two. If he was still unsatisfied he would make a third visit in another month or two. If he was still unsatisfied he would tell the professor point-blank that he was fired. I have often wondered how that would work in a college. Mr. Duke's success in business seems to have been largely due to his ability to select the right men for key positions.

The Trustees of the college appointed a committee of six members "to consider the entire matter of the Duke endowment with reference to Davidson College, in all of its aspects," and to report to the next meeting. The main question to be considered was what use the college was going to make of the income from the Duke endowment. The committee consisted of the following members: W. L. Lingle (chairman), W. J. Martin, W. J. Roddey, R. A. Dunn, J. A. Cannon, and C. M. Richards.

At the meeting of the Trustees on June 2, 1925, this special committee made their report which, in part, reads as follows: "That one-third of the income [from the Duke endowment] be spent on the faculty; that one-third be spent on the general improvement of the plant; and that one-third be set aside to constitute a reserve emergency fund."

The report continued: "Several reasons have led us to make these recommendations. First of all, we do not know how much the annual income from the Duke endowment will be. In the second place we do not know whether it will be the same amount each year. We do know that sometimes industrial corporations have good years, and then again they have poor years. In view of the above facts, it does not seem wise to put the whole of the income into the expansion of the faculty at the beginning. If we should do so, a poor year would leave the college in a bad plight. A gradual expansion, with a reserve emergency fund to provide for a poor year, seems to be a wise policy . . . When we know precisely what the income from the Duke endowment will be, and when we know what we can count on from this source from year to year, we may want to change the policy recommended above."

As I look at that report now in the light of the twenty years that have intervened it seems to me to have been a wise report. But it took no little discussion to arrive at the conclusions reached. I recall that President Martin wanted us to say that no part of the income would ever be used for building purposes. Others of us took the ground that inasmuch as Mr. Duke had put no conditions on his gift, we should certainly not attach any.

On June 1, 1926, the Trustees of the college adopted a plan for retiring professors on an annuity after they had reached the age of sixty-five. The first paragraph of the plan reads as follows: "All members of the faculty and officers of the college shall be retired at the age of sixty-five, subject to annual re-election for further service by the properly constituted authorities."

The annuity plan adopted was that of the Teachers Insurance and Annuity Association of New York, which was founded by Mr. Andrew Carnegie for the purpose of serving retired teachers. Under this plan a member of the faculty or administrative staff authorizes the college to take as much as five per cent out of his monthly salary check. The college then adds to this an equal amount and sends the whole to the Annuity Association. By this process, a comfortable annuity is built up for the beneficiary in the course of years. The adoption of this plan was one of the most forward-looking steps ever taken by the college.

When the income from the Duke endowment began to arrive in amounts ranging from sixty to seventy thousand dollars a year it was apparent that Davidson had reached a new era—an era of expansion along several lines. The administration and Trustees felt the need of expert advice. Dr. Robert L. Kelly, Secretary of the Association of American Colleges, was accordingly employed to make a survey of the college. This he and his assistants did during the session 1925-26. In February, 1926, Dr. Kelly made his report in person to the Trustees. It was afterwards published in the May issue of the magazine, *Christian Education.* The report contained many valuable suggestions which resulted in quite a number of changes in the college.

First of all, the constitution and by-laws of the college were thoroughly revised. In this revision marked changes were made in the organization of the Trustees and of the faculty. For the first time in the history of the college the office of Dean of the Faculty was created. As a result of the income from the Duke endowment and of Dr. Kelly's survey a number of professors were added to the faculty and salaries were increased to meet the increased cost of living.

We may note here that the educational standards of the college were being gradually raised. This is made evident by the fact that Davidson was received into the membership of the Association of Colleges and Secondary Schools of the Southern States in 1921, and was placed on the list of colleges approved by the Association of American Universities in 1922. Additional evidence is seen in the fact that a chapter of Phi Beta Kappa was established at Davidson in 1923. There are no higher educational rating agencies in America than these three organizations.

On November 16, 1926, there occurred an event of first-rate importance, the dedication of the splendid Richardson Athletic Field. This field was constructed by the Richardson brothers, Mr. H. Smith

Richardson, of the class of 1906, and Mr. Lunsford Richardson, Jr., of the class of 1914, as a memorial to their father, Mr. Lunsford Richardson, Sr., of the class of 1875. They presented this field to the college with "the hope that future generations may profit in increasing measure from the benefits of trained minds in strong bodies."

The Richardson brothers have also rendered a large service to the college in many other ways. For twenty years, Mr. H. Smith Richardson was an efficient trustee. Mr. Lunsford Richardson, Jr., also served efficiently as a trustee for a number of years. They both made handsome contributions to the new Chambers Building.

One of the troublesome questions during this era was the problem of getting the fraternities properly housed. The question was before the Trustees time and again, and committees were appointed on several occasions to study the question and recommend solutions for the problem. Several different plans were suggested during the years, but none solved the problem. At length, on February 13, 1928, action was taken by the Executive Committee of the Trustees authorizing the construction of the present Fraternity Court, consisting of eleven small brick buildings costing about $5,000 each, without dormitories, as social centers for the various fraternities. After seventeen years of testing the plan adopted seems to have been the best of all the suggested solutions.

It seems appropriate that I should record here a letter which was addressed to the Greek letter fraternities by the Trustees in May, 1918, during the First World War, as this letter contains principles that members of fraternities should always keep in mind. I prepared this letter at the request of the Trustees. As you read the letter it may be well to keep in mind that I belonged to a fraternity in my college days and am still regarded as a member. The letter reads as follows:

"The Board of Trustees of Davidson College recognizes the good features of Greek letter fraternities, and the valuable service which many fraternity men render to the college. Yet we feel that there are certain tendencies in the fraternity life which need to be guarded against, and that we are just now at the point in the world's history where it becomes our duty to call the attention of our students who are members of fraternities to these tendencies.

"1. The great liberty-loving nations of the world are engaged in a terrible war to make the world safe for democracy. Many men are laying down their lives for this sacred cause. Millions more are ready to lay down their lives. It is a time for all men everywhere to stand for democracy and brotherhood. Our experience and observation lead us to believe that the natural trend of fraternity life is away from democracy and toward exclusiveness. This can be seen by the fact that the social life at commencement and on other public occasions is largely in the hands of fraternity men, and by other similar symptoms. This tendency to exclusiveness does the fraternity man himself real injury. It narrows his friendships and interests, and gives him a point of view which unfits him to do his best out in a world that is standing for democracy. It also works an injustice to the non-fraternity man, and shuts him out from friendships and social life which would be helpful to him. We very earnestly call the attention of our fraternities to this tendency and urge them to guard against it, and to cultivate for themselves and for the college a spirit of democracy which is in keeping with the spirit of democracy and liberty for which we stand in this World War, and which is in keeping with the spirit of Christian brotherhood for which we stand.

"2. There is also a tendency for the fraternity man to make everything revolve around his fraternity, and to be unmindful of the larger life of the college. This is seen at our commencement exercises. When some of the more important events of commencement are taking place, we notice that many fraternity men are gathered about their fraternity halls instead of attending the commencement exercises. This is neglecting the larger college spirit which every student should cultivate. We wish to urge all our students to cultivate the larger college spirit. This will mean much to the students themselves, and a great deal to the college.

"3. We observe the tendency of fraternity men to put the fraternity before the literary societies. In this way these men fail to receive the very best from the literary societies, and from the training which they ought to receive in them, and the literary societies fail to attain to their best. We hope that all fraternity men will diligently guard against this tendency, and that every man in the college will throw himself heart and soul into the work of the literary societies. This is a time when college men need to train for leadership as never before, and the literary societies furnish a valuable part of this training.

"We call upon all fraternity men to watch all tendencies which might result in injury to themselves, to others, and to the college, and to cultivate in all things that large spirit of democracy and brotherhood for which the whole nation is standing and fighting."

In the spring of 1928, right out of the blue, President Martin addressed a letter to the president of the Trustees which in part read as follows: "For both personal and college reasons, I request that the Board of Trustees, at the regular meeting, May 29, 1928, take order to retire me from active service with the college at the close of the session 1928-29." This letter was read to the Trustees on May 29, 1928, but it was all so sudden that the Trustees were at a loss to know what action to take. Therefore, "the whole matter was referred to the Executive Committee, with the authority to work out the details and make any adjustments that may be necessary." There were certain conditions attached to the letter that needed study and further conference. Some members of the Executive Committee, and I was one of them, felt that we should insist upon Dr. Martin's retaining the presidency until he had passed the retiring age named in the annuity plan. Others felt that we should accept his resignation as president, and retain his services as a professor of Chemistry, a possibility mentioned in his letter. We all agreed upon the latter plan and tried to open a position in the Chemistry Department. But the plan did not materialize. There was no need for an extra man in the Department of Chemistry and there were other obstacles.

The final action taken by the Trustees on June 4, 1929, was that his resignation be accepted to take effect on July 1, 1929, that he be made president emeritus, that his full salary be continued for one year longer, and that after that he should receive one-half his salary for the rest of his life. That solution was accepted as satisfactory by President Martin.

At that same meeting the Trustees adopted by a rising vote a handsome tribute to Dr. Martin and his administration covering a typewritten page in the minutes. It was proposed by the president of the Trustees. Here is a paragraph from that tribute: "Dr. Martin is a man of positive Christian character and of strong convictions, and is always ready to stand for the right and against the wrong, no matter what the cost may be to him personally. During his administration the college has made remarkable growth. Under his leadership, supported by an able faculty and an efficient administrative staff, the work of the college has gone forward in a way that we did not suppose was possible seventeen years ago."

Thus closed the longest administration in the history of the college, covering an era that was marked by some shadows, but by many more lights.

X ❧ On Being President

PERHAPS IT MAY be permissible, in the very beginning, to explain how I came to be elected president of Davidson College. Such a personal narration can be justified only by the fact that I am writing my memories and this is certainly one of the most distinct of all the memories that linger. Besides, my election was unexpected and a bit unusual.

Dr. Martin having asked to be relieved of the presidency, the Trustees, on February 20, 1929, appointed the following committee to nominate a new president: Drs. Walter L. Lingle (chairman), Neal L. Anderson, Byron Clark, Robert H. McCaslin, Hamilton W. McKay (M.D.), and Messrs. H. Smith Richardson and S. Clay Williams.

On February 22, as chairman of the committee, I addressed a letter to every member of the faculty and to every trustee, requesting each one to nominate one or more persons for the presidency. In the letter I made the following statements:

"The constitution requires that the president must be a member of some branch of the Presbyterian Church when elected and a member of the Presbyterian Church in the United States (Southern) when inaugurated.

"I feel that the president should have the following three qualifications: First of all, he should be acquainted with the whole subject of college education and its problems. In the second place, he should have executive or administrative ability. In the third place, he should have inspirational power. He will need this in his contact with the students, with the faculty, and with the constituency. It will be difficult to secure a man with all these qualifications, but we ought to get a man who comes as near to them as possible."

About the same time Dr. Hamilton W. McKay, president of the Alumni Association, addressed a similar letter to the alumni of the college asking for nominations.

We received many suggestions in response to these requests. Other suggestions came from those who had seen in the papers that a nominating committee had been appointed. I tabulated all these names suggested. There was a total of forty-six. Although my name was mentioned in a number of letters, I did not place it on the list as I did not think that a man of my age at that time should be elected president of the college, even if there had been no other reasons, and there were others. The nominating committee was called to meet in Greensboro, North Carolina, at two o'clock on Tuesday, April 2, 1929. I promptly placed before the committee the list of forty-six names. We proceeded by the process of elimination. It did not take long to eliminate quite a number. But there still remained quite a list of names that deserved serious consideration. We worked over these until there were only three names left. All three were well-known men who probably did not know that their names were being considered. By the time we had reduced the list to these three it was about six o'clock and we were a bit weary, having been in continuous session for four hours. Somebody accordingly moved that we take recess for fifteen or twenty minutes and then return and complete our work.

As I left the room, a minister who was out of employment was waiting for me and took me into another room where he laid his problems before me at length. I finally had to excuse myself as it was time to resume the committee meeting. Upon my return to the committee room I called the committee to order, and announced that we would proceed and finish our task. I was then informed that the committee had nominated me in my absence. I protested that I was too old for the position and that there were other reasons why I should not think of allowing my name to be presented to the Trustees. Besides, I was greatly embarrassed by the suggestion that while chairman of the committee I should be nominated.

The committee told me that they did not want me to make any decision at that time, but wanted me to think and pray over the matter for a week. But they did want me to resign as chairman of the committee. Of course, there was nothing to do but to resign as chairman, though I remained a member of the committee. Mr. S. Clay Williams was elected chairman.

I thought and prayed over the matter for a week, and then wrote Mr. Williams that I could not consent to my nomination, and urged him and the committee to go ahead and nominate one of the other three men. I did not hear a word from him until May 22. On that date a telegram from Mr. Williams came to me at Montreat where I was attending a meeting of the General Assembly, requesting me to stop over in Greensboro on my way to Richmond. I thought that he wanted to put the finishing touches on the nomination of one of the other three men.

Mr. Williams and one or two other members of the nominating committee met me in Greensboro. They told me that they had met to urge me to allow them to nominate me. They knew that there was a $60,000 debt on a building at the General Assembly's Training School of which I was president, caused by the non-payment of pledges in the Million Dollar Campaign. Feeling that the Training School debt was holding me there, they had passed the collection plate and raised $50,000 to be paid on the Training School debt if I would accept the presidency of Davidson College. That touched me deeply and made a profound impression upon my psychology. I felt that they really wanted me. I told them that I would think and pray over the matter and that if they did not hear from me in twenty-four hours they might present my name to the Trustees, but with the understanding that I could not tell whether I could accept if elected until I knew what happened at both the college and the Training School. That is how I was nominated and elected. The $50,000 was paid to the Training School, but I have never known who paid it. I probably could have found out if I had tried, but I thought it best not to know. However, I am deeply grateful to the donors, whoever they were.

My official connection with Davidson as president began on July 1, 1929, and closed on April 1, 1941. This chapter will, in a general way, cover those years. After I was elected president, a friend, with a twinkle in his eye, said, "You are going to a soft snap. You won't have a thing to do but please the students, the faculty, the trustees, the alumni, the controlling presbyteries, the patrons, the Presbyterian Church at large, and the public in general." I thought of a young minister who became pastor of a large church. A lady who belonged to the church told him that she felt very sorry for him. When he asked why she replied, "You have so many different kinds of people to please." He replied, "I had not thought of it that way. I had thought that if I could only please One [pointing upward] all would be well."

I am also reminded of another incident. At a meeting of the Association of American Colleges about ten years ago saintly Bishop McDowell of the Methodist Church made one of the addresses. He had been a college president in his early days. He began his address by saying, "As I was hurrying to this meeting a friend met me and asked where I was going in such a hurry. I told him that I was on my way to address five hundred college presidents. My friend said, 'Good, maybe you can save some of them.' When I asked what he meant he replied, 'You might save them from their budgets, you might save them from their trustees, and you might even save them from their alumni.' "

No president ever inherited a more loyal or co-operative faculty and administrative staff than I inherited as I entered upon my duties as president of Davidson College. In recently reading over the semi-annual reports that I made to the Trustees during my administration, I was struck with the way in which I referred again and again to the fine spirit of co-operation on the part of the faculty and administrative staff. It made a deep impression on me. So as I refer to various things accomplished during the years of my presidency please let it be understood that I do not claim the whole, or any large part, of the credit. Any credit that is due belongs to the whole group.

President Hoover and I hit upon evil times. We both entered office in 1929, the year of the great financial crash, which marked the beginning of a world-wide depression that lasted for a number of years. I had not been at Davidson two months before the crash occurred on Wall Street and we entered into what was probably the most disastrous financial depression this country has ever known.

Where a Good Past Encourages a Better Future

When I accepted the presidency I had hoped to lead a movement to improve the material equipment of the college. Before I had even moved to Davidson I wrote and requested Dr. J. W. MacConnell, the college physician, to have some ideas and plans to lay before me with reference to a new infirmary. The old infirmary was utterly inadequate. In fact, it was a disgrace. Dr. MacConnell and Mrs. Alice Robson, the nurse, deserve some extra stars in their crown for the fine work they did in that old building. As the country seemed to be prospering, I felt that we could raise money for the new infirmary in a very short time. But when the financial crash came there was no use to talk about raising any considerable sums of money for anything.

However, in 1938, through the generosity of Mr. and Mrs. W. Y. Preyer, of Greensboro, North Carolina, a splendid up-to-date infirmary was erected at a cost of approximately thirty thousand dollars. It was erected in honor of Mrs. Preyer's father, Mr. L. Richardson, of the class of 1875, who learned his first chemistry at Davidson; and of Mrs. Preyer's uncle, Dr. Henry Louis Smith, of the class of 1851, president of Davidson College from 1901 to 1912.

During the depression years our chief business was to keep the college on an even keel. The faculty, students, trustees, alumni, and patrons all felt the effects of the depression. Some felt it very keenly. It was a time of general demoralization. In such a situation we needed to do everything possible to keep the morale of the faculty and students from breaking. Many patrons had such severe financial losses that they no longer had the means to send their sons to college. There was a possibility of there being a serious drop in the number of students. Some valiant work was done by members of the faculty and staff and by the students. As a result there was an increase in the student body. For example, in 1928-1929, the year before the depression, there were 611 students. For the next twelve years the average annual enrollment was approximately 650. In fact, when we reached 650 we fixed that as the limit beyond which we did not want to go for the present. Although we enrolled more than that number at the beginning of several sessions, we did it with the feeling that when the student body got settled down and the usual number had left for one reason or another there would be just about 650. To keep the student body down to that figure we declined to take any students who were in the lower third of their high school classes no matter how many units they had.

The depression years were hard on the finances of the college. Many of those who had borrowed funds from the endowment found it impossible to pay the interest. A little later there was a sharp drop in interest rates. In the meantime, it was necessary to extend more aid than usual to needy students. Under these circumstances many other colleges and universities were cutting salaries right and left and at the same time closing engagements with some of their professors. As stated above, it was a time of general demoralization. Through economy on the part of all and through wise planning on the part of those responsible for the finances of the college, Davidson came through it all without cutting a salary or dismissing a professor.

Notwithstanding the depression, I had the temerity to lay before the Trustees in my report to them on June 3, 1930, a building program that was needed to equip Davidson College for the number of students that we then had and for the work we were trying to do. I will copy the program exactly as it stands in that report:

1. A new infirmary ....$ 40,000.00
2. A new library properly endowed......................   500,000.00
3. A field house or gymnasium.............................   100,000.00
4. A new church 250,000.00
5. A social center in connection with Y.M.C.A.   75,000.00
6. An enlarged chemical laboratory.......................   30,000.00
7. Hard surfaced roads and walks..........................   20,000.00
   (Beautifying the campus)
8. Additional scholarship endowment...................   100,000.00
9. Additional general endowment...........................   500,000.00
10. New dormitory 100,000.00

            TOTAL...$1,715,000.00

I recall that when I had finished presenting this program to the Trustees, one of the Trustees, who was a doubting Thomas, said: "Why didn't you make it a hundred million while you were at it?" The whole thing seemed utterly impossible to him, especially when the entire world was in the depth of a terrible financial depression. Of course I explained that we did not expect to accomplish it all in a period of two or three years, but that it was an ideal toward which we should be working.

It may be proper to pause right here and inquire just how much of this program has been actually realized. In doing this it may be well to keep in mind that during this period there was not only a financial crisis but such an increase in income tax rates as we had not dreamed of. This increase makes it impossible for the friends of the college to give as liberally as they formerly did.

Before my retirement in 1941 I had the pleasure of seeing the following improvements: a splendid new infirmary; a new dormitory; a handsome new library practically completed; the construction of a new science building well under way; large additions made to the seating capacity of the Richardson Athletic Field; a new athletic field graded; the roads within the campus hard-surfaced; many brick and concrete walks laid on the campus; the college laundry practically rebuilt; the sewerage changed from septic tanks, with an outlet through the golf course, to the town sewerage system at a very considerable cost; and many other minor improvements. All the above was fully paid for except the library and science building. The cost of the library was partially paid for and the rest guaranteed by the donor. The science building was only partly paid for. The material improvements mentioned above were made at a cost of approximately $560,000. In the meantime the endowment had been increased by more than $120,000 and $510,000 had been added to trust funds held by others for the college. Thus it will be seen that while good progress was made in my administration, the goal set in 1930 was not fully attained. However, it has been reached and passed during the administration of Dr. Cunningham. More about this later.

Let me state again that I do not claim any large credit for what was accomplished. Others did as much or more than I did. In the final analysis the credit is due to the faculty and staff who by patient and loyal service year after year have made Davidson College an institution that appeals to those who have money to give. Without being invidious I would like to say that especial credit is due to Mr. F. L. Jackson, our Treasurer, for the part he had in helping to secure the funds.

But I have run ahead of my story. Let me come back to the beginning of this period. My inauguration as president of the college took place on June 3, 1930. The program was planned by a committee of which Dr. J. M. McConnell, Dean of the Faculty, was the chairman. It was quite an affair. In fact, it was much more elaborate than I would have planned. Many colleges sent their presidents or other representatives, and the academic procession, with its great variety of hoods, was very colorful and impressive. The following college presidents made brief addresses: Drs. Henry W. Chase, of the University of North Carolina; William Louis Poteat, of Wake Forest College; Davison M. Douglas, of the University of South Carolina; and Benjamin R. Lacy, Jr., of Union Theological Seminary in Virginia. There were also brief addresses by John Calvin Metcalf, of the University of Virginia; Dr. Henry H. Sweets, Secretary of Christian Education of the Presbyterian Church in the United States; and Mr. H. Smith Richardson, president of the Alumni Association. My inaugural address, which was only ten minutes in length, was on "The Place of Personality in Education."

I was scarcely settled in the president's office before problems began to bob up thick and fast. For a while it looked as if there was going to be nothing but problems. First of all was the great brood of problems created by the financial depression. Of these I have already spoken.

Next came the problems connected with the R.O.T.C. and compulsory military training. At that time all students who were physically fit were required to take two years of military training in order to graduate from Davidson. A number of parents besought me to excuse their sons. Some pleaded with me, but I had no power to excuse them.

Then in October, 1929, the Presbyterian Synod of North Carolina passed this resolution: "That the Synod appoint a committee of five ministers and laymen to confer with the Trustees of Davidson College as to the advisability of taking steps to terminate military training at the college." The Synod appointed the committee with Rev. John W. Foster, D.D., pastor of the First Presbyterian Church of Winston-Salem, as chairman. This committee met with the Trustees in February, 1930, and presented with no little earnestness the resolution passed by the Synod. The Trustees appointed a committee to consider the request of the Synod. At the next meeting of the Trustees the whole matter was referred to the Executive Committee. Nothing was done.

In May, 1931, the General Assembly of our Southern Presbyterian Church passed a resolution opposing compulsory military training in our Presbyterian colleges. That brought the college face to face with the question again. In 1932 the Trustees voted to excuse those students who were physically incapacitated, those whose parents were conscientious objectors, and two-year pre-medical students whose schedules were too crowded to take R.O.T.C. But the question would not down. There were still parents who beseiged the president's office and urged that their sons should be excused. Very few of these were conscientious objectors. They felt that their sons could employ their time better on studies that related to their life work. All the while the Trustees and the college administration were under the impression that our contract with the War Department required all students who were physically fit to take two years of military training. As previously stated, the college has nowhere on record the contract with the Government.

As the question kept coming up, I wrote to the War Department and inquired whether the college's contract called for compulsory military training at Davidson and to my surprise got a reply that it did not. With this information before me I made the following recommendation to the Trustees in February, 1934: "That in the future administration of R.O.T.C. at Davidson those students be excused from military training whose parents or legal guardians so request. It is understood that such request must be made in writing and filed with the registrar prior to the opening of the session, and in no case later than ten days after the opening of the session. It is also understood that when a student enters upon the course of military training he is under obligation to take the course for the first two years unless he is excused for physical reasons, or by the military department."

That resolution precipitated one of the warmest debates that I have ever known at a meeting of the Trustees. It was finally approved by a vote of about two to one. One of the most pious ministers that I know was so strongly opposed to the resolution and so wrought up over it that he requested to be excused from asking the blessing at lunch which came immediately after its passage. With the passage of the resolution the whole discussion about military training ceased, after having been a red-hot subject for four or five years. After its passage the parents of ten or fifteen per cent of prospective students requested that their sons should be excused.

It may be proper to state here that I never approved of having R.O.T.C. at Davidson. The Trustees were aware of this when I was elected. My objections were not on conscientious grounds. If they had been, I could not have accepted the presidency. Let me state my reasons briefly. First of all, R.O.T.C. is not in line with objectives for which the college was founded and for which it has been supported all these years. In the second place, the majority of the R.O.T.C. professors do not come up to the academic and religious tests which are required of other professors. After the college requires the most rigid academic and religious tests of its professors, it seems strange that we would ask the Government to keep four or five military professors at Davidson of whom no tests of any kind are required. I used to ask the Government three questions about a prospective military professor: Is he friendly to the Christian religion? Does he use profanity? Does he drink? I always got the reply that the Government had no information about his views or habits.

In the third place, two years of compulsory military tactics and two years of required Bible crowd the schedule so full in the freshman and sophomore years that there is not sufficient time left for those studies that are essential for pre-medical students and for students who plan to enter universities for graduate work. It has been suggested that the college might drop one year of Bible!

In the fourth place, I believe that General Robert E. Lee was right when, as president of Washington College (later Washington and Lee University), he declined to introduce military training, saying, according to Dr. Douglas Freeman in his great biography of Lee, that "Military training is not the best to qualify men for the duties of citizenship, or for success in life."

All of which leads me to the conviction that every church-related college should re-study its objectives from time to time and inquire whether it is really pointing in the direction of those objectives. The faculty and trustees of every church-related college should study their institution from time to time and inquire whether it is in reality a Christian college. They should search their own hearts and try to discover what they can do to make their college more Christian than it is.

The perennial dance problem bobbed up soon after I arrived and like Banquo's ghost would not down. In February, 1930, the Trustees "re-affirmed the historic position of the college concerning social life at Davidson," and called "the attention of the President and Faculty to the importance of protecting the good name of the college in such social gatherings." It is significant that the word "dance" does not occur in the above resolutions. That was the policy of the college at that time. For example, students were not allowed to use the word "dance" in the college paper. In their news articles about dances they used the word entertainment or some similar expression. The Trustees and faculty personally knew that students were holding dances in Charlotte, and sometimes at other placces, but they did not know it officially. Hence no steps were taken to chaperon these dances. There were all sorts of rumors afloat as to misbehavior and drinking at these dances. The rumors were no doubt greatly exaggerated but it was bad for the college to have them circulated. Hence the call upon the faculty to protect the good name of the college.

In February, 1931, the presidents of the student body, senior class, and Y.M.C.A. presented to the Trustees a student petition to be allowed to hold dances at the college. The Trustees appointed a committee to consider the matter. In June, 1931, the Trustees, upon recommendation of the committee, declined to allow dancing at the college, but at the same time addressed an appealing letter to the students. The Trustees also directed the faculty "to take cognizance of the fact that groups of Davidson College students do dance in other places, and to make such restrictions and to throw such safeguards about them as shall be for the best interests of the students and the college."

Again in February, 1935, the students presented another petition to the Trustees to allow them to dance at the college. Again the Trustees appointed a committee, and again, upon the recommendation of the committee, declined. During all these years it seems never to have occurred to the Trustees to ask the advice of the faculty. The Trustees received these petitions directly from the students and made their replies directly to the students. But in February, 1936, a trustee seems to have had a brain-throb, and proposed the following resolution which was promptly adopted: "Resolved that the Trustees go on record as declining to entertain any petitions from the students without the petitions first passing through the hands of the faculty, and that the petitions be accompanied by a recommendation from the faculty which shall guide the Trustees in their action on the petition."

Thus the discussion about dancing went on and on. It caused much unrest among the students and no little criticism pro and con among the patrons of the college and the public in general. Finally in February, 1944, the Trustees put the whole matter of allowing dances at the college into the hands of the faculty by the adoption of the following resolution which was proposed by the faculty: "The faculty of Davidson College recommends to the Trustees that the faculty be authorized to permit dances upon the campus at such times and under such conditions as may be determined by the faculty."

As a matter of course that action has aroused some criticism. To those who look upon the action of the Trustees as an evil thing let me say, if so, then it is the lesser of two evils. Despite all the protection that the faculty could throw around them the student dances in Charlotte had many undesirable features. You can put it down that a large number of young men who come to Davidson are going to dance somewhere. That being true, it is better to have their dances under the immediate control of the faculty. The Davidson College faculty is composed of approximately forty-five fine, sensible Christian men. They are not going to do anything that is radical or that they believe is sinful or improper.

The church problem grew to be a very serious one. The student body outgrew the church building. It was patched and enlarged several times, but even then it was not large enough. Besides, certain sections of it were very uncomfortable. Someone has said that the Lord builds the churches, but sometimes the devil gets the contract for heating, lighting, and ventilating. That saying seems to apply at least to certain areas in the old church at Davidson.

Another problem arose from the fact that there is probably no preacher on earth who can preach in a gripping way every Sunday to 650 students who are required to go to church, especially if a half-dozen different denominations are represented in the student body. So there was a great deal of unrest and criticism concerning the discomforts of the church and the monotony of the services.

An incident comes to mind. Because the church was not large enough for the whole student body, juniors and seniors were allowed to attend either the morning or the evening service, and to hand in cards to their Dean certifying their attendance. It was Mother's Day and a rising senior, who now holds a doctor's degree in English, attended the morning service. The minister did not refer remotely to Mother's Day in any part of the service. Instead he preached about the spiritual qualifications of elders and deacons, as there was an election pending. Now college students have a great deal more sentiment than they are usually willing to admit. When this rising senior handed in his card answering whether he had attended a service, it contained this reply: "Yes, and wasn't it lousy?"

If the Dean had seen that card it might have gone hard with the student. He certainly would not have gotten the assistantship in English for which he was applying. But the secretary to the Dean thought it was so amusing that she brought it to me. I kept it and sent for the student and went over the matter with him and told him that it was never a good plan for a fellow to be just as funny as he could be. He got the assistantship in English. Several years later when a college president asked me to nominate a professor of English I nominated this young man and at the same time told him of the incident. He promptly said that was the man he wanted.

The church problem was solved for the time being by moving the service for the students to the college auditorium in 1936. There every Sunday evening there is a preaching service which all students are required to attend. The most attractive and helpful preachers that can be secured are invited to conduct these services. This is by all odds the most satisfactory arrangement that I have known since I entered Davidson as a student. This service will no doubt be transferred to the new church when it has been erected.

These are but samples of the problems that confront a college president in addition to all the problems connected with the regular duties of the president's office. But let me turn now to some of the things accomplished during that period which I view with more or less satisfaction.

The development of the college library during this period gave me especial satisfaction. A whole book could be written on the evolution of the Davidson College Library. In a report made by a committee of Fayetteville Presbytery in 1844 we find this statement: "The college library is small, and not very valuable. Each of the two literary societies has a library containing about nine hundred volumes." All three of these libraries were located in the old chapel at that time. The libraries of the literary societies were removed to the first floors of the two literary society buildings when they were erected about 1849. When the Old Chambers Building was erected just prior to the Civil War, a spacious front room on the second floor, facing the west, was set apart for the library and the college library was removed thither. The literary society libraries remained on the first floors of their respective halls until 1887.

In 1887, the year before I entered college, the libraries of the literary societies were united with the college library and all the books were carried by the students to the library room in the Old Chambers Building. From that date for a good many years it was known as the Union Library. That was a very spacious room in the Old Chambers, with the ceiling about fifty feet above the floor. There were many windows, but strange to say there was no method of heating or lighting it. When I was a student the library was opened two hours a day, at which time students could withdraw or return books. They never thought of going there to study. In the winter the librarian endured the chill of the room by wearing overcoat and muffler.

In 1909 the Carnegie Library, which has more recently been transformed into the Guest House, was erected. Miss Cornelia Shaw, who had been elected full-time librarian in 1907, took charge and did some heroic work in hammering the library into shape. She continued to hold this position until her retirement in 1937. The college owes to her memory a great debt of gratitude.

It was apparent, when I became president in 1929, that the college had outgrown the library. It had not only outgrown the building, but also the conception that a library is a place to keep books. As I read over the reports that I made twice a year to the Trustees, I am struck with how much I had to say about the need for a new library building, and a new conception of the purpose for which a college library exists. It should be the great central workshop of the whole institution, and an adjunct to every department.

At the suggestion of the Carnegie Corporation of New York, we employed Dr. Louis R. Wilson of the University of North Carolina to make a survey of our library in the fall of 1930. He made many valuable suggestions about the staff, the arrangement of books, and the lighting of the building. Growing out of that survey the Carnegie Corporation gave us $15,000 for books. This was wisely invested by a competent committee of the faculty whose members visited a number of the best college libraries.

The General Education Board became interested and offered to assist a man of our choice in securing the best library education possible in this country, and after that to provide for his salary for a number of years. At the suggestion of Dr. J. M. McConnell, Mr. Chalmers Davidson of the class of 1928, who had taken four years of graduate work at Harvard, was selected. After taking the full library course at the University of Chicago, he was elected Director of the Library and associate professor of Bibliographical History in 1936. Four years later came the munificent gift of Captain James Parks Grey which provided for the erection and support of the Hugh A. and Jane Parks Grey Memorial Library. The books were transferred to this building on October 1, 1941. We now have not only a magnificent building, but a splendid library which has been thoroughly organized and catalogued under the skillful hand of Dr. Chalmers Davidson. Better still, it is fast becoming the central workshop that I hoped it would be.

I look back with considerable satisfaction to the men who were added to the faculty during this period. Here are the names of those who remained for more than one or two years: Dean John C. Bailey, Jr.; Drs. Price H. Gwynn; W. G. McGavock; F. W. Johnston; T. S. Logan; Rene Williamson; J. A. McGeachy; E. E. Brown; Prof. James Christian Pfohl; Mr. Norman W. Shapard, Director of Physical Education; and Mr. Eugene McEver, Head Coach. There were several others who left after a year or two. Of course, some mistakes were made, but for the most part they have corrected themselves. But I submit that the above, taken as a whole, constitute a goodly list. Some of the older members of the faculty have remarked to me more than once that the best thing that was done during my presidency is to be found in the number and character of the men who were added to the faculty. I feel quite sure that the greatest responsibility that rests upon the president of a college is the selection of members of the faculty. It is certainly one of the most difficult things the president of a Christian college has to do.

I also rejoice in the development of the department of music. A large number of students of Davidson College have always loved music, and there have been many and various kinds of student musical organizations in the college. However, it was not until 1926 that a "Professorship of Fine Arts, with especial relation to music" was established. You would certainly expect a liberal arts college to have such a professorship. The first incumbent of that professorship was not entirely satisfactory, and the professorship was temporarily suspended in 1931 until a suitable man could be found. In May, 1933, the Trustees elected Mr. James Christian Pfohl as Director of Music. His position was changed to that of Professor of Music in 1946. Under his leadership the department has developed beyond what we had ever dreamed of, and besides giving the students a musical education has made a deep impression on the public. There are still some who do not believe that music has any place in a college for men. But I cannot agree with them. To my mind music is one of the most cultural of all courses. Of all the many things that I cannot do I would rather play well on some musical instrument.

I look with some satisfaction on what was accomplished in the reorganization of student health service, physical education, and athletics. At a meeting of the Association of American Colleges in 1931 I was struck by an address which President Gates of the University of Pennsylvania made on the plan which they had adopted in that institution. I afterwards had an interview with him in which he explained the plan more fully. When he became president of the University, he appointed a commission to study physical education and athletics in the best institutions of America and Europe. As a result of that study the commission worked out the Pennsylvania plan. I presented this plan to the Trustees of Davidson College. They appointed a committee to study the plan. With some adjustments the plan was adopted by the Trustees in May, 1932, and is fully recorded in the minutes of that meeting.

At a meeting of the Trustees in February, 1940, further marked changes were made. Athletics were made an integral part of the Department of Student Health Service and Physical Education, and the Department "as thus constituted is to be conducted as a regular department of the college in the same general manner in which other departments are conducted." According to the action taken at that time, athletics were put in the hands of the Trustees and faculty, and thereafter directors of physical education and athletic coaches were to be elected by the Trustees and their salaries and terms of office fixed by that body. This was a distinct forward step. The plan is fully set forth in the minutes of the Trustees for February, 1940.

I also take considerable satisfaction in the reorganization of the Public Relations and Alumni Office, and the launching of the Living Endowment. Formerly only those alumni who paid five dollars a year into the Alumni Office were to be considered members of the Alumni Association. The fund thus collected was supposed to support the Alumni Office and secretary, but it never did. The office was directed by the Alumni Association and was not an integral part of the college administration. There were several serious objections to this plan. At the meeting of the Trustees in June, 1938, I proposed a different plan which is set forth in detail in the minutes of that meeting. This plan was approved in principle by the Trustees and was later approved by the Alumni Council. According to this plan all alumni dues were abolished and every man who ever attended Davidson College is to be considered a member of the Alumni Association. The college is to pay all expenses connected with the Alumni Office, which in turn is "to be one of the administrative units of the College under the direction of the College administration."

The following paragraph is an important part of the plan: "Instead of having Alumni dues, let those Alumni who can and will make an annual contribution to the current funds of the College, or to such other funds as the Trustees of the College may suggest, with the understanding that an individual Alumnus may designate his contribution to the department of the College in which he is most deeply interested." That paragraph is the foundation on which our "Living Endowment" is built.

Further action on this plan was taken by the Trustees in June, 1939, including this recommendation in the president's report:

"That you give your approval to the plan known as the 'Living Endowment' as suggested in the paper which you approved in principle a year ago, and as more fully elaborated in a letter which was sent to all Trustees and Alumni last week over the name of the Treasurer of the College. It is our judgment that the plan of the Living Endowment should be associated with the Treasurer's office and not with that of the Alumni office. That you authorize the College Administration, with the approval of the Finance Committee, to secure such assistance for the Treasurer's office as may be needed for the carrying forward of the Living Endowment plan."

Thus came into being the Living Endowment plan, which already means much to the college and should mean more and more as the years go by. The Treasurer of the college deserves great credit for suggestions in connection with the formulation of the plan and for the enthusiastic way in which he has presented it.

The Centennial year, 1937, fell within this period. First of all it was celebrated by the raising of a Centennial Fund for buildings and equipment. A handsome sum was subscribed, but as the two following years were difficult years financially for the whole country, the subscriptions were not as promptly or as fully paid as we had hoped. However, you can see from the building program described in the early part of this chapter that a great deal was really accomplished by this part of the Centennial program and by the publicity given to the needs of the college in connection with it.

In order that the Centennial might be properly celebrated at the commencement of 1937, a committee was appointed, with Professor Archibald Currie as chairman, to plan a suitable program. After much thought and discussion, the committee decided that the most impressive way to celebrate the event would be to put on a great historical pageant, portraying the history of the college from the beginning to the Centennial year. The faculty approved and fixed Monday night of commencement as the time for the pageant.

Mr. Theodore Viehman of New York, a professional producer of pageants, was employed after much investigation. He came to Davidson and spent weeks in studying the history of the college and writing the script for the pageant. A huge stage was erected at the north end of the Richardson Athletic Field. The cast consisted of over 700 persons, and included the whole student body, practically all the members of the faculty, and a number of other people.

The pageant began with the arrival of the Scotch-Irish Presbyterians in the area in which Davidson is located. That involved covered wagons of a very primitive type drawn by oxen or mules. All told, there was a vast amount of paraphernalia. It was all very realistic. Crossing the stage were such historic characters as General William Lee Davidson, General D. H. Hill, Dr. Robert Hall Morrison, Peter Stuart Ney, and Woodrow Wilson, all of whose names are associated with the history of Davidson.

It was a very impressive affair as the rehearsals went on night after night under the floodlights of the Richardson Field. I never saw the students or faculty show more enthusiasm. The publicity concerning the event kept pace with the rehearsals.

At the beginning of the commencement period everything started off finely and everybody was on the tiptoe of expectancy about the pageant, which was to come on Monday night as the climax of commencement. But alas! About five o'clock on Monday afternoon the windows of heaven were opened and the fountains of the great deep were broken up. I don't believe that I ever saw it rain so hard or so long in my life. Telegrams and telephone calls kept coming, inquiring whether we were going to proceed with the pageant. But it was impossible to proceed. So instead of being the climax of commencement it proved to be the anticlimax. Perhaps we shall remember the Centennial year all the better because of the keen disappointment. Whatever else the college got out of the pageant it got some fine publicity. Students and faculty also got a great lesson in teamwork as they worked together and rehearsed together week after week.

In connection with the Centennial celebration the college bestowed an unusual number of honorary degrees. The part that gave me especial pleasure was the conferring of the honorary degree of Doctor of Laws upon Dr. Henry Louis Smith and Dr. William J. Martin, both of whom were former presidents of Davidson College. I like to remember that it was at my suggestion that these two de-

Shearer Hall—Department of Music

grees were conferred. They had many other degrees, but I had a feeling that they would appreciate this degree from their alma mater in the Centennial year quite as much or more than any degrees they already had.

With the passing of the Centennial my thoughts turned toward retirement. In February, 1938, I addressed a letter to the Trustees calling their attention to the fact that I was approaching the age of threescore and ten, and requesting them to appoint a committee to nominate my successor. This letter I placed in the hands of the president of the Trustees. After the Trustees had adjourned I was astonished to learn that he had not presented my letter to the Trustees, as he did not think the time had come for my retirement.

In May, 1938, I addressed another letter to the Trustees in which I again requested that a committee be appointed to nominate my successor, and insisted that this letter be read and put on record. In that letter this paragraph occurs: "I wish to express my appreciation of all the kindnesses and courtesies which the Trustees have shown me. It was a pleasure to work with you as a fellow trustee for twenty-four years [it was really twenty-six] and it has also been a pleasure to work with you as president of the college for nine years [up to that time]. During all these years I have learned to love the college as I have never loved any other institution."

In response to that letter, the Trustees appointed a nominating committee to nominate a new president. After taking plenty of time, and searching far and near, the committee nominated Dr. John R. Cunningham, pastor of the First Presbyterian Church of Winston-Salem, North Carolina, and he was promptly elected. Dr. Cunningham is a native of Missouri, and a graduate of Westminster College, Fulton, Missouri, where the Honorable Winston Churchill made his world-shaking address. Prior to going to Winston-Salem, Dr. Cunningham had been president of the Presbyterian Theological Seminary, Louisville, Kentucky, of which he is an alumnus, for six years. Prior to that he had been pastor of the First Presbyterian Church, Bristol, Tennessee, the seat of King College and other educational institutions. Prior to that he had been pastor of the Presbyterian Church at Gainesville, Florida, the seat of the University of

Florida, with its large student body. Thus it will be seen that he had large experience in working with college students, and considerable experience as president of a theological seminary. From the point of view of personality, education, and experience Dr. Cunningham was eminently fitted for the presidency of Davidson.

Dr. Cunningham began his work as president of Davidson College with enthusiasm and energy on April 1, 1941. It was not long until we all felt that he was the right man in the right place. On the day that Dr. Cunningham took charge I retired, and by action of the Trustees became president emeritus. The day that President Taft left the White House, he said: "I'm glad to be going; this is the loneliest place in the world." I did not feel quite that way about it, but it was an immense relief to have the heavy responsibilities lifted from my heart and mind. Incidentally I may say that being president of a college is a rather lonely job, as it does not seem wise to have intimates either in the faculty or in the student body. Being president emeritus is the most carefree position I have ever held, and thus far it has been a very happy one.

It may be appropriate here to quote, as expressing something of my own experience, a paragraph from Mark Twain, written with a touch of his irrepressible humor, after he had passed threescore and ten. It reads thus: "When I passed the seventieth milestone ten months ago, I instantly realized that I had entered a new country and a new atmosphere. To all the public I was become recognizably old, undeniably old; and from that moment everybody assumed a new attitude to me—a reverent attitude, granted by custom to age— and straightway the stream of generous new privileges began to flow in upon me to refresh my life. Since then I have lived an ideal existence, and I now believe what Choate said last March, and which at the time I did not credit: that the best of life begins at seventy; for then your work is done; you know that you have done your best, let the quality of the work be what it may; that you have earned your holiday—a holiday of peace and contentment—and that henceforth to the setting of your sun nothing will break it, nothing interrupt it."

XI 🐚 From the Window of An Emeritus

THE PRECEDING CHAPTERS have brought my story up to the time of my retirement from the presidency of the college. It is now more than five years since I retired and became an emeritus. Before I proceed to tell something of what has taken place at the college during these five years, please permit a personal word so that you may see the point of view from which I write.

Upon retirement we purchased the old Glasgow residence which is located two hundred yards north of Watts Dormitory. The house has been modernized and made comfortable, and here we dwell under our own vine and fig tree, both figuratively and literally speaking. Our home is ideally located for retirement. In a sense it is remote and quiet, "far from the madding crowd." In another sense it is close in—just across a side street from the college campus. From my study window I can look out upon the college campus and buildings. As I conceive it, the office of emeritus is purely honorary, and carries with it no duties or responsibilities except to wish and pray for the well-being of the present administration and the college. I have kept busy preaching, speaking, and writing during these five years. They have been among the happiest years of my life. They have been made all the happier as I have seen the college go forward so splendidly under the leadership of the present administration. Now let me proceed to tell of some of the things that I have observed from my study window.

Although Dr. Cunningham entered upon the duties of the president's office April 1, 1941, his inauguration did not take place until October of that year. The exercises connected with the inauguration extended over two days. On the evening of October the seventeenth the college gave a dinner in honor of the new president and his wife. Many distinguished guests were present. In connection with the dinner, Dr. Theodore Meyer Greene, professor of Philosophy in Princeton University, made a scholarly address on "The Aim of

Liberal Education." After dinner a brilliant reception was given by Dr. and Mrs. Cunningham in the new Grey Memorial Library.

The official induction of the new president into office took place in the Chambers Auditorium on the morning of October the eighteenth. There were present for this occasion approximately one hundred and twenty-five representatives of the colleges, universities, and educational societies of America. It was a distinguished gathering. The academic procession, consisting of members of the faculty, the Trustees, and the one hundred and twenty-five representative educators, all in academic dress of many colors, was very impressive.

The program connected with the inauguration was as follows: Dr. J. McDowell Richards, president of the Trustees, presided; Dr. Charles E. Diehl, president of Southwestern at Memphis, and Moderator of the General Assembly of the Presbyterian Church in the United States, read the Scriptures; Dr. Daniel S. Gage, professor of Bible and Philosophy in Westminster College, Fulton, Missouri, led in prayer; Dr. John Rood Cunningham was presented for inauguration as the twelfth president of Davidson College by Dr. Walter L. Lingle, president emeritus; the inaugural vows were administered by Dr. Richards, president of the Trustees; Dr. Cunningham made the inaugural address on "Tomorrow and the Church College"; brief addresses of greeting were made by Dr. Henry H. Sweets, of Louisville, representing Christian Education in the Presbyterian Church in the United States; by Dr. Frank P. Graham, president of the University of North Carolina, representing the University System of the State of North Carolina and the North Carolina College Conference; and by Dr. J. R. McCain, president of Agnes Scott College, representing the larger Educational Associations of America. A number of honorary degrees were then conferred. After that the one hundred and twenty-five visiting delegates were presented. The benediction was then pronounced by Dr. Benjamin R. Lacy, Jr., president of Union Theological Seminary in Virginia.

There was one unique feature about this occasion that was never seen before, and will probably never be seen again. Three former presidents of Davidson College were present. They were Dr. Henry

Duke Dormitory

*Chambers Building
from the North Campus*

Louis Smith (1901 to 1912); Dr. William J. Martin (1912-1929); and Dr. Walter L. Lingle (1929-1941).

Every president has what we may call his regular, perennial problems. On top of these he has his special problems. For example, Dr. Martin had World War I, the burning of the Old Chambers Building and Watts Dormitory, and all the problems arising therefrom. President Hoover and I went into office in 1929, and we had scarcely gotten seated in our respective presidential chairs before a worldwide depression hit us broadside. It was about the deepest depression America ever saw, and it kept on and on. There were plenty of problems for the country and for the college. If you don't believe it, ask Mr. Hoover.

Well, the various representatives who provided so much of the pageantry for Dr. Cunningham's inauguration had scarcely gotten home before the United States was plunged into World War II. Only those who were in the thick of it will ever know how many problems that created for the college. The first problem was that of the vanishing student body. The Selective Service Act was passed by Congress and became law on September 20, 1940. By 1941 students and prospective students were being drafted right and left. A glance at the catalogue will show what happened. For the session 1940-41 a total of 678 students were registered. For the session 1944-45 there were only 185 registered, and many of them were drafted during the year. It had been more than forty years since the student body had been that small.

The financial problem became acute at once. With the drop in the number of students, there was a severe drop in revenue. How could the college keep from running a large annual deficit? There was also a problem connected with the faculty. The college did not need forty-five members of the faculty to teach this small number of students. That problem was partially met by allowing some members of the faculty to go to other institutions on lend-lease for the duration, and by retiring some of the older members of the faculty who had reached the retiring age. Still other members went into the active service of the army or navy.

The War Department, in response to a request from the college administration, sent to Davidson a large quota of young men who had applied for admission into the air service, to be given courses in certain subjects. They came in installments of 500. From June, 1943, to June, 1944, there was a total of 2,007 of these air students. Their coming helped to solve the financial problem, but they created a host of other problems. How was the college going to house, feed, and teach them, all of which had to be done under the strictest government restrictions. It had been at least sixty years since the college had maintained a boarding department. A kitchen, which adds nothing to the beauty of the campus or buildings, was erected on the back side of the Chambers Building. Plumbing throughout the dormitories had to be reconstructed to meet the government requirements. Those are just a few of the material problems.

The problem of teaching these air students was even greater. Some of them had not gone beyond high school. Some were college graduates. All had to be taught a few specialized subjects, such as physics, mathematics, geography, history, and English. Where could the college secure a sufficient number of teachers in these branches to teach so large a number of young men? New teachers were brought in. Some of the regular professors taught subjects which they had never taught before. All this was in addition to teaching the regular civilian students. And then they had to make out all sorts of reports, not simply in duplicate, but in quadruplicate, and sometimes more. The professors of Davidson College never worked harder or for longer hours than during this period. It was part of their contribution to the war effort.

These air students were largely from the North and Northwest. I got the impression that for the most part they were fine young men. But there were many names that had a foreign flavor and sounded strange enough in this Scotch-Irish section of the country. Many of them were Roman Catholics, and, strange as it may seem, the Roman Catholic Mass was observed on this Presbyterian campus more than once. Quite a number of these students were married, and some brought their wives along. That resulted in some of the most ardent love scenes on the front of the campus that had ever been witnessed in this proper town, even by the oldest inhabitants. In fact, they became so ardent that the commanding officers had to direct husbands and wives to hold their petting parties in private, or on the back side of the campus.

When all the air students had gone, the War Department sent to Davidson a group of 200 boys under eighteen years of age, to be trained in certain studies preparatory to going into the army. They were known as the ASTRP group—the "Army Special Training Reserve Program." They were all Southern boys, and nice young fellows, but some were very immature and unprepared for college work. Teaching them was quite a problem. This, too, was part of Davidson's contribution to the war effort.

While the college administration and faculty were wrestling with all these problems, there was urgent need for a new gymnasium, a new church, and other material improvements. The fact that the Federal government was pouring billions upon billions of dollars into war industries meant that many people were making more money than they had ever made before. It was an opportune time to raise money. At the cost of much thought and planning, campaigns were organized and set to work. As a result, $250,000 or more was raised for the new gymnasium, and a similar amount for the new church. These buildings will be erected as soon as conditions permit. Unfortunately, owing to a sharp rise in prices, these buildings will cost more than was anticipated.

Funds for other purposes were also secured. The old Carnegie Library was transformed into the Guest House at considerable cost. The Martin Science Building was completed, and the final payments on it were made. There were other minor improvements too numerous to mention, all costing money. A few statistics from the Treasurer's annual report will give some indication of what has been accomplished along financial lines during the present administration. In looking at these statistics we shall have occasion to refer to the "Plant Fund," by which we mean the value of the campus plus the cost of all buildings and equipment, plus the funds on hand for building purposes.

In April, 1941, the endowment was......................$1,073,000.00
By April, 1946, it had reached............................. 1,256,000.00
In April, 1941, the plant fund stood at.................. 1,794,000.00
By April, 1946, it had reached............................. 2,565,000.00

In April, 1941, trust funds held by others for the college amounted to $570,000. By April, 1946, these trust funds amounted to $790,-000. A little computation shows that there was a total increase of $954,000 in the endowment and plant funds between 1941 and 1946, to say nothing of unpaid pledges, and of the increase of $220,000 in the trust funds held for the college by others.

Now let us go back a little. In 1930 I mapped out a program for the college which called for an estimated outlay of $1,715,000, whereupon a trustee whistled, and asked why I had not made it a hundred million. Since 1930 the plant and endowment funds have increased $1,600,000, and the trust funds held by others have increased $730,000. This does not include the bequest from the estate of the late Col. E. L. Baxter Davidson, of the class of 1881, a lifelong friend of the college. It is estimated that this bequest will amount to approximately a half-million dollars when the estate has been settled. Thus it will be seen that the goal set in 1930 has been reached and passed.

I mention all these things for the encouragement of doubting Thomases who seem staggered by the large programs for the college which are mapped out from time to time. Those who are responsible for the well-being of our church-related institutions should take for their motto the one that William Carey, the great missionary, formulated a hundred and fifty years ago: "Undertake great things for God. Expect great things from God."

While all this was going on, Davidson students were going out into the uttermost parts of the world to fight and die in behalf of human freedom. A total of 2,536 students and alumni, and nine members of the faculty and staff, entered the service. One hundred and fifty of these made the supreme sacrifice. Two hundred and twenty-nine others suffered wounds. Many honors came to Davidson students and alumni who were in the service. Fifteen hundred of them became commissioned officers. A total of seven hundred and six decorations were awarded to them. It is interesting to note that 136 Davidson alumni went as physicians and dentists, and 89 went as chaplains. My heart has been deeply moved by the death of so many of our former students who went into the service. Many of them I knew and loved as if they had been members of my own family. We earnestly hope and pray that the sacrifices that were made, both by the living and the dead, may not be in vain, but that there may come out of it all a new and better world, in which there shall be peace and justice and righteousness.

From my window I have seen many changes in the faculty since my retirement. The following members have been called to their eternal reward: Drs. W. J. Martin, W. R. Grey, Archibald Currie, H. B. Arbuckle, Frazer Hood, and S. C. Lyon. The following have retired: Drs. M. E. Sentelle, J. M. Douglas, C. M. Richards, W. L. Porter, and J. W. MacConnell. Dr. Price H. Gwynn has resigned and moved to Philadelphia. Other younger men who had not been here so long have accepted positions in other institutions. When I look at the above list of names I think of the cry of Elisha as he saw Elijah taken up: "My father, my father, the chariot of Israel, and the horsemen thereof." I think of those men as constituting the Old Guard. Their places will be hard to fill. Reverting to Elijah, we can only hope that a double portion of their spirit may fall upon those who are called to succeed them.

Marked changes have also taken place in the administrative staff during these five years. Dr. C. K. Brown is Dean of the Faculty, with his office next to the president's office. After the death of Dean J. M. McConnell in April, 1935, I requested the Trustees to elect a Dean of the Faculty to take his place, but some influential members of the Trustees objected, as they thought the next president should have the privilege of nominating his own dean. The next president did not come for six years, and I had to limp along without a dean. However, at the suggestion of the same trustees I selected Professor John C. Bailey to give me such assistance as he could in an unofficial way, and I am still grateful for the help that he gave.

Professor Bailey is now Dean of Students, and occupies Dr. Sentelle's former office. A portrait of Dr. Sentelle hangs on the wall as a kind of guardian angel for him. From all reports he is doing a swell job. He actually signs all his letters, of which there are many. The familiar "dictated but not read" at the bottom of letters has disappeared.

A great change has taken place in the Alumni and Public Relations Office, and I am going to take a wee bit of the credit for it, as I helped to pave the way in the manner referred to in the preceding chapter. Mr. John L. Payne, of the class of 1916, is secretary. Being a man of large business experience he has the office organized in a very efficient way, with a number of helpers doing secretarial work.

There are some faces that I greatly miss from the administration staff. Miss Hattie Thompson, who became assistant to the Treasurer in 1918, retired in 1945. She was brought up in the town of Davidson and probably knew more alumni than anyone else connected with the college. Mrs. N. T. Smith, who began her service as Supervisor of the Dormitories in 1922, retired in 1943. She will be remembered affectionately by many former students. I also miss the quick, sparkling repartee of Mrs. Adele Arbuckle Logan, who was secretary to the Treasurer for quite a number of years, but resigned last year and married Dr. Thomas S. Logan of the Department of Chemistry. I miss, too, the radiant face of Miss Dorothy Finlayson, who was secretary to the Dean of Students for a good many years, and is now Mrs. Moreland Cunningham.

But there are still quite a number of old-timers in the Administrative Department who help to give continuity to the life of the college. There is Mr. F. L. Jackson, who became Treasurer of the college in 1912, and has made one of the most efficient treasurers any college ever had. Associated with him is Mr. Myron W. McGill, the Auditor, who has been associated with the college ever since his graduation in 1922, and who can do more work and make less noise about it than almost any man I ever saw. At the other end of the Administrative Row is Mr. Fred W. Hengeveld, who became Registrar in 1921. As Secretary of the Faculty for years, he probably signed more diplomas than anybody else ever connected with the college, except myself. As president of the Trustees from 1906 to 1929, and president of the college from 1929 to 1941, I probably hold the record for the number of diplomas signed. Mr. Hengeveld did some strenuous work and rendered a large service as member of the draft board during World War II. Miss Orrie Steele, who has the distinction of having been secretary to three different presidents of Davidson College, is still filling that office with efficiency. I venture to say that all three presidents, if they could speak, would say that no president ever had a more loyal secretary, or a more faithful one. Not only so, but she knows how to keep silent in seven languages concerning the things she sees in the stream of correspondence that passes through her hands. She also has the gift of meeting the public in a gracious manner.

I would like to pay tribute to the large number of men who work with their hands as caretakers and campus workers. Some of them have been with the college for many years. Among them are some of the finest Christian men I have ever known. Someone has said that if you want to know whether a college is Christian or not, ask the janitors and scrubwomen. They know.

Marked changes are taking place on the campus, as well as in the personnel of the college. Some time ago Mr. Charles F. Gillette, a well-known landscape architect of Richmond, Virginia, was employed to make a survey of the campus and then make recommendations as to the placing of future buildings, and as to ways and means of beautifying the campus. The fact that he is a Presbyterian elder gave him special interest in the college. From my window I can see things that are already taking place as a result of his recommendations. Here are some of them:

The Morrison Hall, which was built as a gymnasium and Y.M.C.A. hall in my student days, has been removed. I have some happy memories connected with that old building. The first floor was used for roller skating, and we used to take our best girls there and skate by the hour. Other happy memories are connected with the Y.M.C.A. work that was conducted on the second floor.

The old wooden barracks, known as North and South, which were erected to meet an emergency when the Old Chambers Building was burned in 1921, have also been removed. All the trees in that area have been cut down. The entire area that lies between the Chambers Building and East and West and Duke Dormitories has been graded to the level of the rest of the campus. Duke Dormitory and the Richardson Athletic Field are now plainly visible from the front of the campus. This vision gives a sense of unity to the grounds and buildings, and adds much to the attractiveness of the campus.

Nine hundred and eleven students entered Davidson in September, 1946. That is very nearly fifty per cent more than the college registered prior to the war. It has meant crowding in the dormitories. The college has admitted that number of students as an emergency measure to help in relieving a situation that exists in all the colleges and universities of America. Judging from what took place after World War I, I venture to predict that there will be a large number of applications for several years, and perhaps permanently. That instantly raises the question of how many students Davidson should take, as a permanent proposition.

Prior to World War I there were many among the trustees, alumni, and friends who felt that Davidson should limit the student body to about three hundred. A larger number might detract something from the traditions and ideals of the college. After the war the student body shot to 600 almost over night. Then we set 650 as the limit, and stuck to it until World War II. So far as I could see, the spirit and ideals of the college were just as fine with 650 as they had been with 300, or even with 100. Now the question arises as to whether the college can safely go beyond the 650 mark. To my way of thinking that depends upon at least three things. First of all it depends upon the type of students to be admitted. The college can safely take more students who rate high in character and intellectual preparation. In the second place it depends upon the size of the faculty. The college cannot safely take more students than the faculty can teach effectively. In the third place it depends upon the housing facilities. The students cannot do their best work when they are crowded in their rooms or classrooms. If these conditions are

Martin Science Building

met, it seems to me that Davidson can safely take more than 650 students without doing injury to its ideals and traditions. At any rate, one generation cannot fix for the next generation the exact number of students the college may enroll.

Now a word about the students as I look from my window in the spring of 1947. At the end of the first semester some graduated; others dropped out for various reasons, and a number of new students entered. The catalogue for this session shows a total of 971 students. At present there are approximately 900 in actual attendance. More than double this number have applied for entrance in September, 1947.

The students are more mature both in their looks and in their ways than any student body I have ever known. Many of them are ex-service men. Large student bodies can become very noisy at times, especially toward the fag end of the session. I live where I can hear any undue noises in and around the dormitories. I have heard no such noises this year. All's quiet on the western front. Better evidence of their seriousness is to be seen in the college library, especially at night. When I visit the library at night I see a great many students hard at work, poring over books and encyclopedias and taking notes. Nothing delights my heart more. In working to secure a new library I said again and again that the library should be the central workshop for the whole college. The Grey Memorial Library is fast becoming that. As the ex-service men continue to return to college during the next few years I expect to see this seriousness of purpose continue and deepen.

It can be seen from the foregoing that the president has plenty to do, and that he has been doing a plenty. But I have scarcely touched upon his greatest and most responsible task. His greatest and most responsible task does not consist in raising money, erecting buildings, and in providing material equipment, as important as all that may be, but in building the faculty. Great inroads have been made in the faculty by death, retirements, and resignations, and it has to be virtually rebuilt. From experience I know how difficult it is to find professors who will fit into the ideals and requirements of Davidson College. The future of the college depends upon securing the right men. Dr. Cunningham seems to have been very successful along this line thus far. The following new professors have been added to the faculty to fill vacancies, and to provide for the increased student body: George L. Abernethy, Ph.D., professor of Philosophy; C. J. Pientenpol, Ph.D., professor of Physics; William Olin Puckett, Ph.D., professor of Biology; James F. Pinkney, LL.B., professor of Political Science; Bradley D. Thompson, M.A., associate professor of History; Edward O. Guerrant, Ph.D., associate professor of International Relations; A. G. Griffin, M.A., associate professor of Economics; Gordon Wood, Ph.D., assistant professor of English; William S. Connor, M.S., assistant professor of Economics; Albert C. Winn, B.D., assistant professor of Bible; James M. Robinson, B.D., assistant professor of Greek and Bible; Pedro N. Trakas, M.A., assistant professor of Romance Languages; Claude L. Ives, M.A., assistant professor of Education; John D. Haldane, Jr., B.M., assistant professor of Music; J. N. Behrman, B.S., assistant professor of Economics; Ralph L. Sparrow, instructor in Mathematics; Stanley A. Rhodes, M.A., instructor in Biology; Melvin B. Winstead, B.S., instructor in Chemistry; and James Cogswell, B.D., assistant in the department of Bible.

It is high time for these memories and observations to come to an end. However, I cannot close without speaking of some of the emotions that well up in my heart as I think back over the years to 1888 when I entered Davidson as a freshman. First of all there is a deep sense of gratitude for the privilege that I have had of being intimately associated with the students, faculty, administrative staff, trustees, alumni, and friends of Davidson College for more than half a century. If all these could be brought together in one body, they would make a great group of noble men and women. They have left a deep impression upon my life and character. Whatever I may or may not have meant to Davidson College in the official positions that I have occupied, Davidson College and these associations which I have had, have meant vastly more to me. I owe a debt that I can never repay.

When I think of the college as I first knew it in 1888, and then look at it today, an indescribable feeling comes over me. The development of Davidson College over the years has been one of the most amazing things that has come within my observation during a long life. There are only four buildings on the campus that were here in my student days—the quaint little dormitories known as Elm Row and Oak Row, and the two literary society halls. All the splendid buildings that adorn the campus today have been erected since I was a student. In the meantime the endowment and income of the college have increased far beyond anything that was dreamed of in those days. The student body is more than ten times as large as it was in 1888. The faculty is seven or eight times as large as it was then. The curriculum has been greatly enlarged, and the academic standards have been raised. Back in the earlier years, friends were afraid that the college would lose something of its soul if it should ever grow larger. Their fears have not been justified. The Davidson spirit which I felt at my first commencement still abides, and has grown even stronger and finer. Renewed emphasis is being placed upon the spiritual as well as the educational mission of the college.

As my imagination goes back to the beginning in 1837 and comes down through the years trying to visualize all those who had a part in making Davidson College I can see a great multitude of men and women, numbering thousands and tens of thousands, who by their lives, labors, prayers, and contributions have been used of the Lord in making Davidson College what it is today. As my mind thus travels over the years my feelings are best expressed in the words of that first telegram: "What hath God wrought!"